STRENGTHENING CROSS-BORDER COMMUNITY COLLABORATION IN THE CAREC REGION

A SCOPING STUDY

DECEMBER 2020

ASIAN DEVELOPMENT BANK

Contents

Figure, Tables, and Boxes

Preface

The Central Asia Regional Economic Cooperation (CAREC) Program is a partnership of 11 countries—Afghanistan, Azerbaijan, the People's Republic of China, Georgia, Kazakhstan, the Kyrgyz Republic, Mongolia, Pakistan, Tajikistan, Turkmenistan, and Uzbekistan—and development partners, working together to promote development through cooperation, leading to accelerated economic growth and poverty reduction.

The CAREC 2030 strategy was endorsed at the 16th Ministerial Conference in October 2017 and marked a new era for the program toward 2030. It envisions a mission to connect people, policies, and projects for shared and sustainable development, serving as the premier economic and social cooperation platform for the region. CAREC selectively expanded its operational priorities under the new strategy to better address the region's development needs and help its member countries achieve the 2030 Global Development Agenda.

Some CAREC member countries have experienced high economic growth, but development across the CAREC region has not been even. The region faces many political, economic, social, and environmental challenges that directly impact citizens and communities. To further expand opportunities in the region and realize its potential for continued economic growth inclusively, CAREC member countries must work as a community to address these common and interrelated challenges. Enhancing people-to-people contacts across countries and promoting collaboration among cross-border communities, youth, women, and small and medium-sized enterprises would contribute to the region's sustainable growth.

This study assesses the current dynamics of border communities' collaboration in the CAREC region and identifies opportunities for promoting community development and people-to-people contacts.

Acknowledgments

This study was undertaken by the Central Asia Regional Economic Cooperation (CAREC) Secretariat and the Asian Development Bank. The team would like to thank Werner Liepach, director general, Central and West Asia Department; and Safdar Parvez, director, Regional Cooperation and Operations Coordination Division, Central and West Asia Department, for overall guidance.

The CAREC Secretariat at Asian Development Bank managed the production of this scoping study. The Secretariat team supporting CAREC border communities work includes Saad Paracha, senior regional cooperation specialist and CAREC unit head; Laura Izquierdo, regional cooperation specialist; and Irene S. de Roma, programs officer. The team would also like to extend its gratitude to Guoliang Wu, principal results management specialist, who was CAREC unit head when work on this study started.

The team expresses its appreciation to the regional cooperation coordinators and national focal points' advisors of all CAREC countries for the assistance extended in collecting relevant information from their respective countries.

This study's principal author is Haris Q. Khan, who built on the work started by Pervaiz Ahmed.

Abbreviations

ADB	Asian Development Bank
AKDN	Aga Khan Development Network
ASEAN	Association of Southeast Asian Nations
AU	African Union
CAREC	Central Asia Regional Economic Cooperation
CSO	civil society organization
EAPTC	Eastern Partnership Territorial Cooperation
EU	European Union
GIZ	Deutsche Gesellschaft für Internationale Zusammenarbeit
ICT	information and communication technology
km	kilometer
MSMEs	micro, small, and medium-sized enterprises
PATRIP	Pakistan–Afghanistan–Tajikistan Regional Integration Program
PRC	People's Republic of China
SDG	Sustainable Development Goal
SWOT	strengths, weaknesses, opportunities, and threats
UN	United Nations
UNDP	United Nations Development Programme
WUA	water user association

Executive Summary

1. Introduction

In October 2017, the Central Asia Regional Economic Cooperation (CAREC) Program approved a new strategy, CAREC 2030, with the mission "to connect people, policies, and projects for shared and sustainable development." CAREC 2030 groups activities into five operational clusters, including a new cluster on human development, and commits to fostering economic and social cooperation among cross-border communities.

This study aims to assess how CAREC, as a regional cooperation platform, can promote closer economic and social cooperation and people-to-people contacts among border communities and propose directions and opportunities for scaling up cross-border community development initiatives in the region.

While the formal function of a border is to control and restrict the movement of people and goods, cross-border communities in the CAREC region have interacted for trade, labor, health care, and education for centuries, developing connections and creating the potential for greater regional cooperation and shared economic growth.

2. CAREC Region

CAREC countries occupy a wide geographic territory comprising thousands of kilometers, share borders, and have deep historical and cultural ties. Yet they speak various languages and represent political, economic, and ethnic differences. Geopolitically, the 11 CAREC countries are members of different and, only partly, overlapping regional groupings and programs.

Although CAREC borders have their unique characteristics, they have certain common barriers to enhanced people movement across borders. These barriers include inadequate physical infrastructure, made particularly acute given the vast distances and difficult geography and access in some countries; restrictive visa and border control procedures; limited cross-border cooperation instruments as well as participation between border and local administrative bodies; and cross-border security and instability, often due to control over natural resources.

In addition, women living in bordering areas face specific difficulties. Generally, gender disparities remain in border communities like in other areas of CAREC countries and are even more severe, given the peripheral status of these areas. These disparities include areas such as (i) access to decent work, economic opportunities, education and training, health services, information and communication technology (ICT), infrastructure, and public services; and (ii) participation in decision-making processes.

3.   Current State of Cross-Border Community Cooperation in the CAREC Region

The CAREC region has multiple borders representing diverse communities, with unique historical legacies and sociopolitical environments. The dynamics of border communities' interaction between CAREC countries are marked by several factors such as the political and socioeconomic context of countries that they border with, the length of these common borders, the regulations at formal and informal border crossing points, the ethnic background of communities, and the nature of economic activities and opportunities in the border regions. Given this diversity, this study takes a border-specific approach in analyzing cross-border communities' cooperation and dynamics of people-to-people contacts over five selected borders in the CAREC region: (i) Afghanistan and Pakistan; (ii) Afghanistan and Tajikistan; (iii) Azerbaijan and Georgia; (iv) the People's Republic of China (PRC) and Mongolia; and (v) borders in the Fergana Valley (the Kyrgyz Republic, Tajikistan, and Uzbekistan). These borders have been selected to represent the geographic variations in the CAREC region, demonstrate different stages of development in cross-border community collaboration, and highlight the varying sectoral focus and institutional support mechanisms for border communities in the region.

(i)   **Afghanistan and Pakistan**. This border stretches 2,430 kilometers (km), where ethnic groups such as the Pashtuns live across both sides of the border and maintain close contact, owing to their traditional cultural, linguistic, and economic ties. In addition to livelihood-related interactions—both formal and informal, and often provided by extensive trade networks—border communities also rely on cross-border commuting to access education and health care. Some promising cross-border initiatives give hope for integration. For example, the Pakistan–Afghanistan–Tajikistan Regional Integration Program (PATRIP) Foundation built health care facilities in Khyber Pakhtunkhwa and Balochistan provinces in Pakistan, which also serve Afghan border communities. Cross-border trade markets in the Torkham and Wesh–Chaman crossing points offer border communities economic opportunities and possibilities to engage in trade and business. Youth exchanges through universities and youth centers are also a proven tool to increase contacts and cross-border cooperation and integration between the two countries.

(ii)   **Afghanistan and Tajikistan**. Afghanistan also borders Tajikistan to the north, sharing 1,206 km along the Amu Darya, Pyanj, and Pamir rivers. Agriculture provides the main source of income for those living in border areas on both sides. It depends on transport connectivity, access to markets, and reliable availability of water, reinforcing the need for regional cooperation. Regional cooperation is also necessary, given that agricultural communities on both sides of the border are prone to natural disasters such as floods and landslides. Security and instability also remain a major concern for border communities with organized crime and illegal trade activities. Initiatives such as the Border Management Programme in Central Asia and the Livelihood Improvement in Tajik–Afghan Cross-Border Areas have been implemented by the United Nations Development Programme (UNDP) to fight these challenges. Several infrastructure projects carried out by the Aga Khan Development Network (AKDN) have also improved border communities' access to markets and health-care facilities and facilitated exchanges of knowledge and ideas between people from both countries.

(iii)   **Azerbaijan and Georgia**. These countries share 480 km of common borders. Border communities living in the Azerbaijani side often cross to Georgia to buy products and to avail of private health services. Tourism has increased between these two countries and bordering regions such as Kakheti and Kvemo Kartli (Georgia) and Ganja, Sheki, and Gabala (Azerbaijan), offering good conditions for joint development of touristic sites. Agriculture, more specifically production of grapes for winemaking, also plays a dominant role in this bordering region and offers opportunities to develop joint initiatives for border communities. The border region between Lagodekhi (Georgia) and Balakan (Azerbaijan) provides a good example of successful cross-border cooperation, as the local municipalities jointly organize cultural and sports events. Effective initiatives to promote border communities include those implemented under the Eastern Partnership Territorial Cooperation Support Programme. The program aimed at empowering young people living in cross-border regions by increasing their employability skills through training and communication between potential employers and beneficiaries. It also aimed to increase tourism potential in bordering regions, improve agricultural pest control in bordering areas, and facilitate the integration of children with disabilities living in border regions through joint training courses and awareness campaigns.

(iv) **People's Republic of China and Mongolia**. Mongolia borders to the south with two autonomous regions of the PRC—Xinjiang Uygur Autonomous Region and Inner Mongolia Autonomous Region—sharing 4,600 km of borders. Border communities' residents on the Mongolia side often cross the border into the PRC, seeking medical care and work opportunities in industries such as arts, media, and sports. The crossing point between Erenhot (Inner Mongolia) and Zamyn-Uud (Mongolia) has an economic cooperation zone, a duty-free trading facility where border communities can sell local products. The increase in tourism between these countries could positively impact the livelihoods of border communities, boosting the development of related industries such as transport, catering, and entertainment.

(v) **Fergana Valley (Kyrgyz Republic, Tajikistan, and Uzbekistan)**. The Kyrgyz Republic shares 984 km with Tajikistan and 1,314 km with Uzbekistan. Tajikistan has 1,312 km of common borders with Uzbekistan. The Fergana Valley crisscrosses these three countries, bringing together communities from parts of Batken, Jalal-Abad, and Osh oblasts (regions) in the Kyrgyz Republic; Soghd Region in Tajikistan; and Andijan, Fergana, Kokand, and Namangan in Uzbekistan. Cross-border interaction between community members happens through formal and informal trading, and common use of water and pastures. These interactions are encouraged by a visa-free regime and help strengthen trust between communities, improve relationships, and establish cross-border networks. However, competition over natural resources and the securitization of borders still cause occasional conflicts between border communities in the valley. Nevertheless, there are successful stories of community collaboration. For example, the Kara-Suu market of Osh oblast in the Kyrgyz Republic has promoted border communities' mobility in the region. Border communities sell their products in the market, with customers and agricultural and other products supply from Uzbekistan. The Ferghana Valley Rural Enterprise Development Project supports micro, small, and medium-sized enterprises (MSMEs) in rural border areas of the Fergana Valley; aims to strengthen linkages in supply chains; and facilitates greater access to markets across borders.

As the above examples suggest, cross border cooperation can significantly improve border communities' livelihood opportunities and increase their access to social services. Successful community collaboration programs have been implemented along and across CAREC borders and cover a wide range of areas, ranging from enhancing trading activities to tourism, from educational exchanges to improved access to health care. However, these programs need to be scaled up and made more sustainable.

4.   International Best Practices on Border Community Cooperation

Experiences from international institutions in promoting cross-border community collaboration were analyzed to build on these findings. From a global and historical perspective, CAREC countries are not unique in their desire to create a more unified region and community. Diverse regions have achieved this unity while dealing with challenges that are not different from those faced by CAREC countries today, such as divergent approaches to cross-border cooperation and differences in languages, ethnicity, religious traditions, and economic development.

Lessons from institutions such as the European Union (EU), the Nordic Council, the Association of Southeast Asian Nations (ASEAN), and the African Union (AU) are relevant for CAREC regional cooperation initiatives on border communities' development. For example, European countries upgraded infrastructure to reduce border barriers and enhance cross-border cooperation, and they established associations (e.g., the Association of European Border Regions) to strengthen regional cooperation. Additionally, the Nordic European experience shows that it is possible to develop meaningful regional cooperation between very diverse countries. ASEAN experiences demonstrate that local institutional structures could be strengthened to effectively increase people mobility across borders. Finally, the AU shows that progressive and selected institutional partnerships could increase the scope, scale, and sustainability of cross-border initiatives.

5.   Strengths, Weaknesses, Opportunities, and Threats Analysis

Despite some progress, the scope for expanding cross-border community collaboration remains enormous, particularly if some of the identified physical barriers and policy and regulatory bottlenecks can be addressed. This report provides a brief strengths, weaknesses, opportunities, and threats (SWOT) analysis of the scope for CAREC to strengthen cross-border communities' development.

(i)   **Strengths**. The CAREC Program is a well-established regional cooperation platform that actively engages with governments. It focuses on investments and policy dialogue on sectors—such as connectivity, trade, education, tourism, health, and agriculture—that have great potential to promote people-to-people connectivity. Border communities in the CAREC region often share traditional cultural, linguistic, and economic ties that lay the groundwork for integrated initiatives.

(ii)   **Opportunities**. CAREC can use cross-border infrastructure projects across the region to boost border communities' development. ICT helps speed up processes in border crossing points and allows e-commerce. The use of ICT can be increased with CAREC support for communities' development. CAREC can further utilize formal and informal trade networks across borders to promote trade initiatives. The regional trend toward easing visa regulations can facilitate border community contacts and allow increased travel and transit. The rich cultural heritage offers potential for cross-border tourism, which CAREC can help develop. Economic cooperation zones projects in the region can be expanded, as well as the related industrial development in border areas. Potential CAREC support to MSMEs in border areas can increase economic opportunities. CAREC can partner with other institutions interested in supporting cross-border community development. Existing and ongoing studies by CAREC on several sectors, such as education, tourism, health, or agriculture, offer an important modality to propose and adapt recommendations for border communities' development.

(iii)   **Weaknesses**. CAREC activities for cross-border community development can be hindered by the peripheral status of border regions with no major policy influence in capitals. Development challenges can be overwhelming due to high rates of unemployment in border areas. More weaknesses include poor public service delivery in border regions, such as in education or health care; limited people mobility due to limited infrastructure, visa restrictions, and security environment; incompatible legal and administrative systems across borders; insufficient coordination and information sharing by border management agencies; limited cross-border institutions to ensure strategic and effective cross-border movements of goods and people; varying state-to-state relations; and patriarchal sociocultural practices that hinder women from fully participating in economic activities in border areas.

(iv)   **Threats**. Climate change effects will be experienced, particularly in border areas prone to natural disasters such as floods. Competition over natural resources may cause conflicts between bordering communities. Political instability and pandemics, such as the coronavirus disease, can cause borders to lockdown.

6.   Recommendations for CAREC

This study identifies a series of recommendations for CAREC to play a proactive role in expanding cross-border cooperation in the border regions, based on lessons learned from international best practices and the findings of the SWOT analysis. Planned CAREC initiatives should pay attention to realizing the potential for regional cooperation through promoting cross-border community collaboration in various sectors and areas. These recommendations can be implemented by adopting a community-driven approach and grouped into three categories: (i) sector-specific recommendations, (ii) institutional recommendations, and (iii) gender equality recommendations.

Proposed recommendations include conducting studies to increase the understanding of specific features in borders, such as border management, agricultural value chains, disaster management, and existing cross-border institutions for border communities' development, including those tackling gender issues. Recommendations also include conducting regional forums, conferences, and fairs for networking and sharing knowledge and experiences. A set of recommendations is also provided to support the development of gender-inclusive policies and establish effective regional mechanisms to promote border communities, such as a regional chamber of commerce working group and a regional tour operators association. Capacity building for border-communities, border institutions, and officials through trainings and programs is also recommended.

ADB and other CAREC development partners could provide technical assistance as a start to facilitate dialogue and prepare robust project proposals to deepen community collaboration in the region. The CAREC Institute could also provide support in undertaking research, trainings, and data dissemination relating to cross-border community collaboration.

1. Introduction

1.1. CAREC and CAREC 2030 Strategy

1.   The Central Asia Regional Economic Cooperation (CAREC) Program is a partnership of 11 countries[1] and development partners that work together to promote development through cooperation, leading to accelerated economic growth and poverty reduction.

2.   Endorsed by the 16th Ministerial Conference in October 2017, the CAREC 2030 Strategy provides a long-term strategic framework with the mission to connect people, policies, and projects for shared and sustainable development in the region. One of the important outcomes of this effort is promoting regional cooperation and integration to include effective dialogue and increased people-to-people exchanges throughout the region.[2]

3.   Part of this new long-term strategy is CAREC moving toward establishing itself as a regional platform with a broader mandate that includes helping its member countries achieve the 2030 Global Development Agenda, the Sustainable Development Goals (SDGs), and the Paris Agreement reached at the 21st Conference of the Parties to the United Nations (UN) Framework Convention on Climate Change. CAREC's regional approach to cross-border community development directly targets four of the 17 SDGs:

   (i)   **SDG 8: Decent work and economic growth**—Promote inclusive and sustainable economic growth, employment, and decent work for all.
   (ii)   **SDG 9: Industry, innovation and infrastructure**—Build resilient infrastructure, promote sustainable industrialization, and foster innovation.
   (iii) **SDG 10: Reduced inequalities**—Reduce inequalities within and among countries.
   (iv)   **SDG 11: Sustainable cities and communities**—Make cities and human settlements inclusive, safe, resilient, and sustainable.

1.2. Scoping Study Purpose, Methodology, and Structure

Purpose

4.   The study aims to assess how CAREC, as a regional cooperation platform, can promote closer economic and social cooperation and people-to-people contacts among border communities and

---

[1]   The CAREC member countries are Afghanistan, Azerbaijan, Georgia, Kazakhstan, the Kyrgyz Republic, Mongolia, Pakistan, the People's Republic of China (PRC), Tajikistan, Turkmenistan, and Uzbekistan.

[2]   CAREC. 2017. *CAREC 2030: Connecting the Region for Shared and Sustainable Development.* Manila.

propose directions and opportunities for scaling up cross-border community development initiatives in the region.

Methodology

5.   The study overviews all CAREC border areas and selects five key borders to examine the national and regional programs and plans aimed at (i) creating a favorable environment to overcome the marginalization of border regions, and (ii) developing a collective perspective on cross-border regional development. The study suggests development initiatives by identifying shared problems of cross-border communities in the border regions of CAREC countries and highlights opportunities to enhance people-to-people contacts and realize regional common development potential.

6.   The research approach is based on strengths, weaknesses, opportunities, and threats (SWOT) analysis to identify general development opportunities and priorities to utilize strengths and reduce weaknesses. This analysis will help develop initiatives with specific priorities in terms of quality, time, and fields of activity.

7.   The study uses both quantitative and qualitative research methods to detail cross-border communities. Secondary research includes demographic surveys, academic journals, policy notes, donor reports, intergovernmental agreements, and regional frameworks. The thematic areas covered in the literature review include social development (health, education, community-driven development, economic development, and civil society strengthening); infrastructure (cross-border infrastructure activities, including roads, bridges, and energy); economic development (business to business, cross-border markets, trade, and enterprise development); tourism; natural resource management; agriculture and farmers' organizations, including water user associations (WUAs); border management; and disaster risk management. CAREC work in other fields, such as tourism, education, health, and economic corridors development, is also revised to ensure alignment between past and ongoing work and proposed recommendations in this study.

8.   Field missions are conducted in Azerbaijan, the People's Republic of China (PRC), Georgia, Mongolia, and Tajikistan to expand secondary research. Meetings are held with stakeholders related to cross-border communities' development initiatives, such as donors, implementing agencies, development partners, government officials and local administrations, academic institutions, private enterprises, and civil society organizations (CSOs). The missions also include field visits to cross-border infrastructure projects, including bridges, markets, border crossing points, and mutual economic zones (Appendix 1).

Structure and Scope

9.   The study is structured in six sections. After the introduction, the context is set in section 2 by describing the diversity of CAREC nations, the barriers to cross-border communities' collaboration and enhanced people-to-people contacts, and women's role in border communities.

10.   Section 3 takes stock of the current overall state of cross-border community cooperation in the region and selects five borders, which represent the geographic variations in the CAREC region, to assess in detail: (i) Afghanistan and Pakistan; (ii) Afghanistan and Tajikistan; (iii) Azerbaijan and Georgia;

(iv) Mongolia and the People's Republic of China;[3] and (v) the Fergana Valley (the Kyrgyz Republic, Tajikistan, and Uzbekistan).

11.   Section 4 identifies lessons learned from and best practices in cross-border cooperation across the globe.

12.   Section 5 undertakes a SWOT analysis of the scope for CAREC to support cross-border community development, followed by an outline of how the region and the program strengths can promote people-to-people connectivity, how to translate opportunities into initiatives for cross-border communities' development, and how to address weaknesses and threats.

13.   Section 6 concludes by offering a series of recommendations for CAREC to support border communities' development and increase people-to-people contacts in the region, pointing out potential partners and borders that should be prioritized.

1.3. People-to-People and Border and Cross-Border Communities' Approach

14.   While the most evident function of a border is to act as a barrier and instrument for controlling the movement of people and goods, borders can also impact regional development, given their frequent role of hosting border communities. These communities form because a border is utilized, legally or illegally, for (i) obtaining resources regularly, such as work, supplies, trade, or education; and (ii) maintaining connections across the border for other economic or personal reasons. In this context, the phrase "cross-border communities" is used throughout this study to refer to people who live close to national borders and systematically cross them for the reasons mentioned.

15.   Cross-border communities can positively impact the regional development process if they are supported with special economic policies and a community-positive ("people-to-people") approach that leads to establishing a common border region identity, generation of social capital, and strengthened trust between border communities living on both sides of the border. In simpler terms, one can think of "people-to-people" as neighbors being friendly and kind toward each other and having convenient and legal ways and places to interact and exchange value so that the entire neighborhood grows prosperous and stays safe.

---

[3]   The provinces of Xinjiang Uygur Autonomous Region and Inner Mongolia Autonomous Region in the PRC are part of the CAREC region.

2. CAREC Region

2.1. CAREC Countries Diversity

16.	CAREC countries occupy a wide geographic territory, comprising thousands of kilometers (km), share borders, and have deep historical and cultural ties. Yet they speak various languages and have political, economic, and ethnic differences. Geopolitically, the 11 CAREC countries are members of different, and only partly, overlapping regional groupings and programs. For example, Azerbaijan, Georgia, and Kazakhstan are members of the European Higher Education Area or Bologna Process.[4] Kazakhstan and the Kyrgyz Republic joined the Eurasian Economic Union.[5] Afghanistan and Pakistan are members of the South Asian Association for Regional Cooperation.

17.	The CAREC region consists of countries with varying income levels: upper middle-income countries (Azerbaijan, the PRC, Kazakhstan, and Turkmenistan); lower middle-income countries (Georgia, the Kyrgyz Republic, Mongolia, Pakistan, and Uzbekistan); and low-income countries (Afghanistan and Tajikistan). Likewise, the proportion of CAREC countries' population living below national poverty line also differs from one country to another (Figure 1). Some have an acute economic dependence on natural resources—e.g., Azerbaijan, Kazakhstan, and Turkmenistan, being major petroleum exporters; and the PRC, being highly reliant on petroleum imports.

18.	The varying income levels in the CAREC region have resulted in divergent patterns of cross-border labor movement. For instance, Kazakhstan is a net importer of labor, mainly from neighboring countries, while Afghan border communities rely on the daily wage labor market on the Pakistan–Afghanistan cross-border transit points. Inner Mongolia Autonomous Region in the PRC offers employment and livelihood opportunities for Mongolian border communities.

19.	All these aspects contribute to defining the identity of border communities, their interaction dynamics, and the barriers to enhanced people's movement across borders.

4	Asian Development Bank (ADB). 2019. *Education and Skills Development under the CAREC Program: Scoping Study*. Manila.

5	The Eurasian Economic Union is an international economic union which has been established as a free trade zone that allows free movement of goods, services, capital, and people and pursues coordinated, harmonized, and single policies.

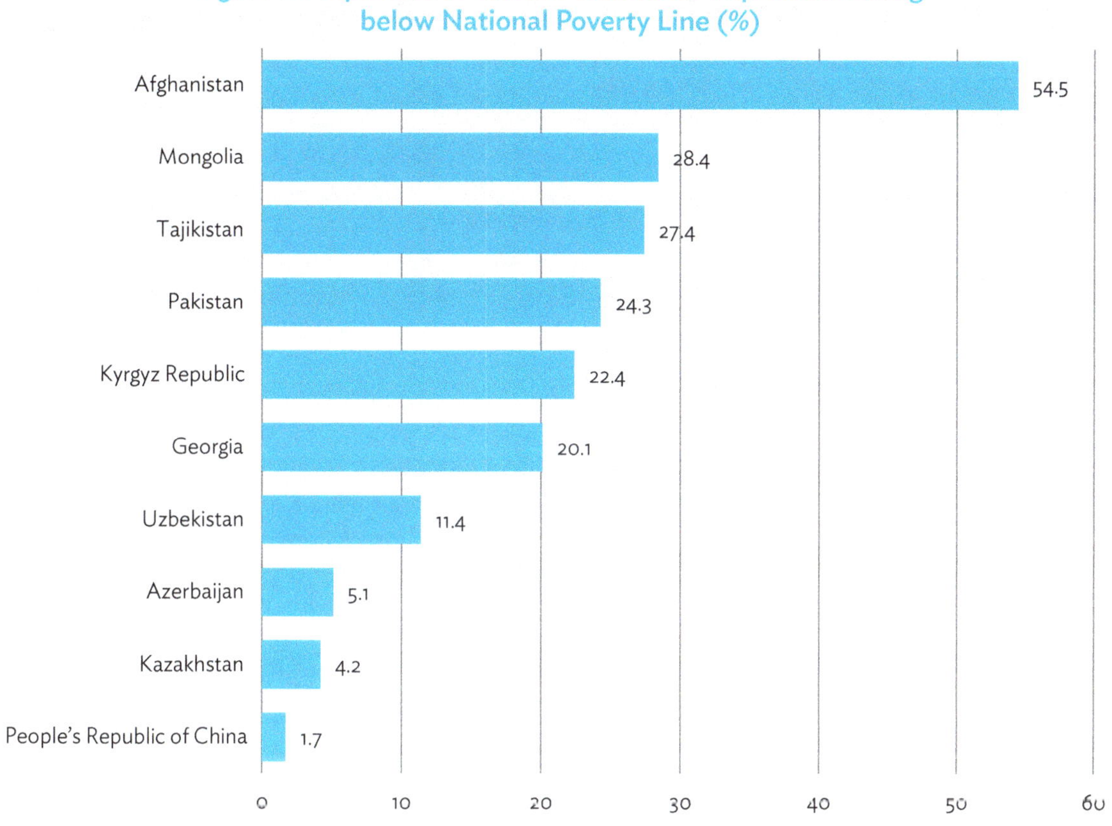

Figure 1: Proportion of CAREC Countries' Population Living below National Poverty Line (%)

Notes: Data are from 2018, except for Pakistan (2015), Afghanistan (2016), and Kazakhstan (2019). No data are available for Turkmenistan. Data for the People's Republic of China differ from standard definition or refer to only some parts of the country. Data for Uzbekistan refer to preliminary figures.

Source: Asian Development Bank. 2020. *Basic 2020 Statistics*. Manila.

2.2. Barriers to Cross-Border Communities' Development and Enhanced People-to-People Contacts

20.   Border areas play an important role in the cross-border political economy and people-to-people contacts. Dynamics in borders are contingent on institutional frameworks, reflecting the interest of national policies, technical and physical barriers, and standards held in different countries.[6] Although CAREC borders have unique characteristics, they have certain common barriers to enhanced people's movement across borders, such as the following:

(i)   **Inadequate physical infrastructure**. CAREC countries are characterized by vast distances with difficult access, and many of the region's borders are equally hard to cross due to mountainous or remote terrain. These factors contribute to high costs of physical connectivity in the region and limited people-to-people contacts.

---

[6]   H. Coccossis and P. Nijkamp, eds. 2012. Overcoming Isolation: Information and Transportation Networks in Development Strategies for Peripheral Areas. In *Advances in Spatial Science*. Springer Science & Business Media. p. 55.

(ii) **Restrictive visa and border control procedures**. Each CAREC member country uses its own system of visa and border entry arrangements. Visa obtention is subject to various requirements between CAREC countries and depends on the origin of the CAREC visitors (Appendix 2). Significant progress has been made by many CAREC countries in reducing the entry requirements for foreign and CAREC country visitors. For example, Uzbekistan launched the 30-day visa waiver to 45 countries (from 1 February 2019), and Pakistan plans to ease visa restrictions for visitors from 55 countries. In addition, the system of border controls at almost all land border crossings frequently involves lengthy queues and processing times.[7]

(iii) **Limited cross-border cooperation instruments**. The participation of border and local administrative bodies is limited in the management of cross-border programs. More generally, no dedicated instruments of public law are valid throughout the CAREC region for managing cross-border cooperation. However, some local administrative bodies participate in cross-border cooperation initiatives. For example, the International Center for Boundary Cooperation opened in the PRC–Kazakhstan border in 2011, which serves as a duty- and visa-free zone for citizens of both countries. Also, the Irkeshtam Pass development serves as a gate for goods between the PRC and the Kyrgyz Republic. In addition, Uzbekistan's decision to allow micro traders to cross the country's borders has led to the cottage industry spurring in areas like the Fergana Valley, where Uzbekistan, the Kyrgyz Republic, and Tajikistan intertwine.

(iv) **Cross-border security and instability**. Border areas sometimes suffer from insecurity and instability, often due to control over natural resources, which ultimately hinder people-to-people contacts across borders and, therefore, communities' development. Border security situation in the CAREC region has improved to some extent over the years. Skirmishes between border guards of CAREC member countries are rare. Moreover, changes in Uzbekistan's foreign policy at the end of 2016 brought positive impetus to the whole regional security environment.

2.3. Women in CAREC Border Communities

21.   Women living in CAREC bordering areas face specific difficulties, apart from the barriers mentioned. As members of border communities, women also cross the border regularly to (i) obtain access to different resources such as work, supplies, trade, education, or health; or (ii) maintain personal connections with family and friends. The frequency with which women cross the border is increased, as childcare is widely considered women's responsibility; women cross the border seeking services for their children too.

22.   Generally, gender disparities remain in border communities like in other areas of CAREC countries regarding participation in decision-making processes and access to decent work, economic opportunities, education and training, health services, information and communication technology (ICT), infrastructure, and public services. More specifically, there is a systemic gender gap in labor force participation, with differences in employment rates, pay scales, and quality of employment. There are also gender biases in hiring practices and promotion opportunities, and failure to implement national policies on flexible working arrangements, parental leave, and equal pay. In addition, female entrepreneurship is undermined in many countries by factors that include lack of finances for start-ups and expansion because of women's

---

7   ADB. 2019. *Promoting Regional Tourism Cooperation under CAREC 2030: A Scoping Study*. Manila.

limited ownership of assets to leverage credit. Women's political participation in all CAREC countries falls well below the 33% advocated by the Beijing Platform for Action,[8] and the proportion of women in senior management positions remains low. Women are also often among the most affected by external shocks such as drought or flooding linked to climate change, food and oil price fluctuations, and global pandemics such as the coronavirus disease (COVID-19) because of their disproportionate exposure to risk and primary care responsibilities.[9]

23.	The peripheral status of bordering areas makes these disparities even more acute for women living in the CAREC border regions and creates additional difficulties. For example, informal and small-scale trading activities are a major source of income for many women living in the borders. In doing so, women tend to travel on foot, making them vulnerable to harassment or abuse. They are also less informed about market rules, making them more likely to become targets of harassment and extortion, impacting their well-being and cutting into their time and profits. Women in CAREC countries often have the primary responsibility for household water management and are thus disproportionately burdened by water supply and quality issues. Water management in borders is more challenging, as water resources are divided by international borders, creating an additional burden for women.[10]

24.	Several initiatives have been launched toward strengthening women's role in border communities' development in CAREC countries. For example, the Cross-Border Cooperation for Sustainable Peace and Development project in the border between the Kyrgyz Republic and Tajikistan helped women strengthen their skills in conflict prevention, negotiation, and peacebuilding.[11] Data show that when women take part in peace negotiation processes, agreements' probability to last at least 15 years increases by 35%.[12]

---

[8]	The Beijing Declaration and Platform for Action was endorsed at the Fourth World Conference on Women of the United Nations (UN) in Beijing in 1995. It recognizes women's rights as human rights and sets out a comprehensive road map for achieving equality between women and men. See UN Women. Beijing Platform for Action.

[9]	CAREC Gender Assessment is being formulated to serve as a base and provide major inputs for the CAREC Gender Strategy 2030. It aims to increase the potential and capacity of women to benefit equally from CAREC investments and to have equal access to any opportunities. It also supports national and regional efforts in addressing gender disparities. ADB. Draft CAREC Gender Strategy 2030. Unpublished.

[10]	H. S. Warren, M. Liungman, and A. Yang. 2019. What's It Like for Women to Trade across Borders? World Bank Blog. 3 June.

[11]	The project was launched in December 2015 by UN Women, World Food Programme, Food and Agriculture Organization, UN Children's Fund (UNICEF), and United Nations Development Programme (UNDP). It was funded by the UN Peacebuilding Support Office and the Swiss Agency for Development and Cooperation. See F. de Weijer. 2017. *Review of PBF Cross-Border Cooperation for Sustainable Peace and Development*. PeaceNexus Foundation.

[12]	UN Women. 2017. *Women Forge Peace along the Kyrgyz-Tajik Border*. Stories. 2 February.

3. Current State of Cross-Border Community Cooperation in the CAREC Region

3.1. Overview of CAREC Borders

25.   CAREC border regions are not only vast in their geographic span but also complex in their composition, as communities live between two societies, cultures, and economic systems that may be altered by the changing landscape of international relations. The region has multiple borders representing very diverse communities, with unique historical legacies and current political and socioeconomic contexts.

26.   The dynamics of border communities' interaction between CAREC countries are marked by several factors such as the political and socioeconomic context of the countries they border with, the length of these common borders, the regulations at formal and informal border crossing points, the ethnic background of communities, and the nature of economic activities and opportunities in the border regions.

27.   Countries such as Azerbaijan with Georgia, and Mongolia with the PRC only border with one CAREC country; the PRC, in contrast, borders with six CAREC countries: Afghanistan, Kazakhstan, Mongolia, the Kyrgyz Republic, Pakistan, and Tajikistan.

28.   The length of these common borders varies significantly between member countries. The border of around 70 km between Afghanistan and the PRC is the shortest, far from over 4,600 km border between the PRC and Mongolia.

29.   There are formal (official) and informal (unofficial) crossing points along these kilometers of borders. While some countries have just a few official crossing points, such as Kazakhstan with Turkmenistan, others have more than 10, which is Uzbekistan's case with the Kyrgyz Republic and Tajikistan. In addition, informal border crossing points can often be found all along the region, more commonly in the border between Afghanistan and Pakistan. Enclaves in the region—such as Sarvan, a small territory of Tajikistan within Uzbekistan—add complexity to the CAREC border network.

30.   In addition, communities in the CAREC borders are not ethnically homogenous. Kazakhstan, for example, boasts more than 100 different ethnic groups, with the Kazakhs, the Uzbeks, the Kyrgyz, the Tajiks, the Turkmens, and the Russians being the dominant groups.

31.   Borders bring together different economic activities and people interaction, successfully happening, for example, in the Kara-Suu market of Osh region in the Kyrgyz Republic border with the PRC. Border markets bring product specialization, such as agricultural, mining, or handicraft industries in the Caucasus and Pakistan border with Afghanistan.

32.	These differences between CAREC borders can be harnessed to develop initiatives for economic development across sectors analyzed in this study. Table 1 summarizes the main official border crossing points between CAREC countries. Further details of these borders can be found in Appendix 3.

Table 1: Border Crossing Points between CAREC Countries

Country 1	Country 2	Km of Border	#	Name of Crossing Point	#	Name of Crossing Point
AZE	GEO	480	1	Red Bridge	4	Mughanlo or Samtatskaro
			2	Sadikhli or Vakhtangisi	5	Almali or Gardabani
			3	Balakan or Lagodekhi		
AFG	PRC	76	1	Wakhjir Pass		
			2	Tegermansu Pass		
	PAK	2,430	1	Torkham		
			2	Spin Boldak (Wesh–Chaman)		
			3	Ghulam Khan		
	TAJ	1,206	1	Shir Khan Bandar–Panji Poyon		
			2	Sultan Ishkashim		
	TKM	744	1	Torghundi–Serkhetabat		
			2	Aqina–Ymamnazar		
	UZB	137	1	Hairatan–Termez		
			2	Hairatan–Galaba		
PRC	KAZ	1,533	1	Khorgos–Nur Zholy	4	Dostyk/Druzhba–Alashankou
			2	Maikapchagai–Jeminay	5	Qaljat (Kalzhat)–Dulata Port
			3	Bakhty–Tacheng		
	KGZ	858	1	Irkeshtam Pass: Osh–Kashgar		
			2	Torugart Pass		
	MON	4,677	1	Erenhot–Zamyn Uud	4	Sheveekhuren–Sekhee
			2	Bulgan–Takashiken	5	Sumber–Arxa/Aershan
			3	Bichigt Zuun–Khatavch		
	PAK	438	1	Khunjerab Pass		
	TAJ	477	1	Kulma Pass (Karasu Pass)		
KAZ	KGZ	1,212	1	Korday	4	Aisha Bibi–Chon-Kapka
			2	Karasu or Ak-Tilek	5	Sypatay Batyr
			3	Kegen	6	Chaldovar
	TKM	413	1	Zhanaozen–Garabogaz		
			2	Bolashak–Serkhetyaka		
	UZB	2,330	1	Zhibek-Joly–Gisht Kupric	5	Kaplanbek–Zangiota
			2	Tejen–Daut Ata	6	Atamaken–Gulistan
			3	Yalama–Konysbayeva	7	Celinny–Ak Oltin
			4	Serke-Turkistan (Kazygurt)–Tashkent	8	Sirdarya–Malik

continued on next page

Table 1 *continued*

Country 1	Country 2	Km of Border	#	Name of Crossing Point	#	Name of Crossing Point
KGZ	TAJ	984	1	Batken–Isfara	4	Karamyk–Daroot Korgan
			2	Kulundu–Ovchi Kalacha	5	Bor-Doba–Kyzylart
			3	Madaniyat–Madaniyay		
	UZB	1,314	1	Dostyk–Dostlik	6	Kara-Bagish–Mingtepa
			2	Bekabad–Khanobad	7	Baymak–Kasansoy
			3	Madaniyat–Madaniyat	8	Seydukum–Pushmon
			4	Kizil-Kiya–Uzbekistan	9	Intimak–Keakaner
			5	Kensay–Uchkurgan	10	Sumsar–Karakurgan
TAJ	UZB	1,312	1	Aivaj–Gulbakhor	7	Khashtyak–Bekabad
			2	Bratstvo–Sariasiya	8	Novbunyod–Pap
			3	Fatehabad–Oybek	9	Kushtegirmon–Plotina
			4	Patar–Anderkhan	10	Zafarabad–Khavasabad
			5	Sarazm–Jartepa	11	Khavatog–Uchkurgan
			6	Rawat	12	Urta-Tepa–Kushkent
TKM	UZB	1,793	1	Farap–Alat	4	Doshoguz–Shavat
			2	Telimerjen–Talimarjan	5	Kunya-Urgench–Khujayli
			3	Gasojak–Drujba	6	Farap–Khojadavlet

AFG = Afghanistan, AZE = Azerbaijan, PRC = People's Republic of China, GEO = Georgia, KAZ = Kazakhstan, KGZ = Kyrgyz Republic, km = kilometer, MON = Mongolia, PAK = Pakistan, TAJ = Tajikistan, TKM =Turkmenistan, UZB = Uzbekistan.

Note: Countries are ordered alphabetically, and each border appears only once.

Source: CAREC Secretariat.

3.2. Assessment of Five Selected CAREC Borders

33.　　Given the diversity of the CAREC border regions, this study takes a border-specific approach in analyzing cross-border communities' cooperation and dynamics of people-to-people contacts. This analysis is based on geography, bordering regions characteristics, history, socioeconomic and labor market dynamics, and regional infrastructure projects. National and regional programs that support people connectivity across borders and cross-border communities' development have also been identified. Given the complexities that an analysis of all the CAREC region borders would generate, only five borders have been selected: (i) Afghanistan and Pakistan; (ii) Afghanistan and Tajikistan; (iii) Azerbaijan and Georgia; (iv) the PRC and Mongolia; and (v) the Fergana Valley (the Kyrgyz Republic, Tajikistan, and Uzbekistan). These borders have been selected to represent the geographic variations in the CAREC region, demonstrate that cross-border community collaboration is at different development stages, and highlight the varying sector focus and the institutional support mechanisms for border communities in the region.

(i.)　Afghanistan and Pakistan Border

34.　　The border region between Afghanistan and Pakistan stretches 2,430 km. Ethnic groups, such as the Pashtuns, live across both sides of the border, representing more than 4 million living in the districts bordering Afghanistan in Khyber Pakhtunkhwa, Pakistan.[13] People on both sides of the border have maintained close contact, owing to their traditional cultural, linguistic, and economic ties (Box 1).

---

[13]　Free and Fair Election Network. 2019. *Peaceful, Well-Managed Elections in Newly Merged Districts Mark Completion of Constitutional Merger.*

35.   Extensive **trade networks**, both formal and informal, run across this border. For example, through the Torkham and Wesh–Chaman[14] border crossing point, wholesale goods are imported and then distributed to retail markets across Afghanistan. Despite the limited infrastructure, the region border markets offer border communities economic opportunities to engage in trade and business. Evidence shows that many Afghans cross the border at least once a year, and about 20% of them conduct regular business with residents in Pakistan in addition to family members. Community and households often depend on such trade for their economic welfare.[15]

Box 1: Deep Cultural Ties between Afghans and Pakistanis

Haider Khan is a 35-year-old man who is part of the Pashtun Shinwari clan based in the Khyber valleys and the Spingar (White Mountain) in the Afghanistan–Pakistan border. His family lives in the Pakistan side of the border, and he works in Kabul, Afghanistan as a cook. He said, "I travel to Pakistan every week. I leave Kabul every Thursday and come back on Saturday." Khan, like most people who cross this border on a regular basis, does not have travel documents. He trusts his tribal connections and cultural bonds will grant him an unhindered journey.

Source: S. K. Saif. 2016. *Why the Border Can't Separate Afghan and Pakistani Pashtuns. DW.* 3 June.

36.   Border communities, particularly in Afghanistan, rely on cross-border commuting in addition to livelihood-related interactions to access **education and health care**. With limited tertiary health-care facilities in Afghanistan, and above all in the peripheral border areas, most Afghan border residents need to travel to Peshawar, Pakistan for medical care.

37.   There are already promising cross-border initiatives that give hope for future integration of border regions. For example, the **Pakistan–Afghanistan–Tajikistan Regional Integration Program (PATRIP) Foundation**[16] has funded several social and economic infrastructure projects in partnership with Wish International,[17] Sarhad Rural Support Programme,[18] and Balochistan Rural Support Programme[19] in some bordering districts of Khyber Pakhtunkhwa and Balochistan provinces in Pakistan. For instance, it built health-care facilities in Dir and Bannu districts of Khyber Pakhtunkhwa, which also serve people on the other side of Afghanistan's border. Another landmark infrastructure project completed by PATRIP is the **Pak-Afghan Joint Trade Centre** in Chaman, a town on the Pakistan side of the border with Kandahar province, Afghanistan, which facilitates information and knowledge sharing among traders and businesspeople from border communities.

---

[14]   The Wesh–Chaman border crossing joins the town of Chaman in Balochistan (Pakistan) and Wesh in Spin Boldak, Kandahar province (Afghanistan).

[15]   A. Morel. 2020. Afghanistan's Borderlands: Unruly, Unruled, and Central to Peace. *The Asia Foundation.* 22 January. The study looked into livelihoods and trade in Afghanistan, specifically in Spin Boldak in Kandahar province, Muhmand Dara in Nangarhar province, the two districts in Torkham, and Wesh–Chaman.

[16]   PATRIP Foundation was funded in November 2011 by KfW, the German state-owned development bank. Its aim is to promote integration and enhance cross-border cooperation and exchange between Afghanistan and its neighbors, Pakistan and Tajikistan.

[17]   Wish International is a national nongovernment organization mainly working in the tribal areas of Khyber Pakhtunkhwa bordering with Afghanistan.

[18]   Sarhad Rural Support Programme is a nonprofit, nongovernment organization working in Khyber Pakhtunkhwa and parts of Federally Administered Tribal Areas. Community empowerment and economic and livelihood development are the program's principal approaches.

[19]   It is a nonprofit, nongovernment organization working in the rural areas of Balochistan. It was funded by the German technical cooperation agency Deutsche Gesellschaft für Internationale Zusammenarbeit (GIZ) in 1983 under the name of Pak-German Self Help Project, and recalled as Balochistan Rural Support Programme in 1991.

38. Similarly, in Kurram district in Pakistan, **Sarhad Rural Support Programme** has completed several projects such as schools for Pakistani and Afghan children and linked roads between the two countries, providing access to education and other services to border communities.

39. In addition, youth exchanges are a proven tool for cross-border cooperation and integration. Many Afghan youths study in Pakistani universities and form close links with their Pakistani peers. Several **youth centers** have been established, such as those by Balochistan Rural Support Programme in Chaman and Nushki in Pakistan, the Center for Research and Security Studies in Pakistan, and the Afghan Studies Center.[20] They have engaged thousands of youth from both countries in several sports events, resulting in large-scale contacts. The **Pak-Afghan Youth Dialogue** by Afghan Studies Center can be highlighted as a good practice that provides "a platform for the youth of Pakistan and Afghanistan to interact on issues of bilateral concerns, exchange ideas and become messengers of peace and cooperation beyond boundaries."[21]

(ii.) Afghanistan and Tajikistan Border

40. The border between Afghanistan and Tajikistan stretches 1,206 km, from Uzbekistan's tripoint in the west until the PRC in the east. The Amu Darya, Pyanj, and Pamir rivers draw this border almost entirely, except for the Wakhan Corridor Section in the easternmost part of Afghanistan.

41. **Agriculture** provides the main source of income for those living in border areas on both sides. It depends on transport connectivity and access to markets, as well as reliable availability of water and land, reinforcing the need for regional cooperation—e.g., Ishkashim border market (Box 2). These needs are even more acute in border areas vulnerable to natural disasters such as floods or landslides.

Box 2: Ishkashim Border Market: "No Man's Land" between Afghanistan and Tajikistan

The Panj River defines the border between Ishkashim, Afghanistan, and the Tajikistan town of the same name on the other side. As the river is considered a "no man's land," it can easily be accessed by both Afghans and Tajiks so long as they return to their respective countries after the visit. In the center of the Panj River is the Ishkashim Market, a border bazaar. It is a strip of neutral ground where locals from both countries come together to trade.

Source: Atlas Obscura. Ishkashim Border Market.

42. **Border security and instability** are major concerns for border communities due to organized crime and illegal trade activities. To fight these challenges, the United Nations Development Programme (UNDP), with European Union (EU) funding, launched the **Border Management Programme in Central Asia** in 2003. This program aimed to enhance security and facilitate trade in Kazakhstan, the Kyrgyz Republic, Tajikistan, Turkmenistan, and Uzbekistan. Based on lessons learned from this project, the EU is also providing similar support to Afghanistan for capacity building of border management agencies and infrastructure upgrade. UNDP is also implementing a similar integrated border management program

---

[20] The Afghan Studies Center is an initiative by the Center for Research and Security Studies in Islamabad, Pakistan. This center is an independent and nonprofit think tank and advocacy center whose aim is to promote academic, cultural, and sports exchanges between neighboring communities from Pakistan and Afghanistan.

[21] Afghan Studies Center. Pak-Afghan Youth Dialogue Series.

called **Border Management in Northern Afghanistan**.[22] The project has contributed to improving the capacity of the Afghan Border Police to secure Afghanistan's borders through capacity building, improved internal coordination, and enhanced collaboration across borders. Both programs are critical interventions to control borders and improve infrastructure services at the border crossing points to promote legal movement of people and cross-border trade.

43.   Another project implemented by UNDP is **Livelihood Improvement in Tajik–Afghan Cross-Border Areas**.[23] The geographic areas covered under this project during the first phase were eight districts of Khatlon province of Tajikistan. In Afghanistan, the project was implemented in the district Imam Sahib in Kunduz province and Dasht-e Qala and Yangi Qala districts of Takhar province to support equitable development and growth through income-generating activities.

44.   The **Aga Khan Development Network (AKDN)**[24] is a prominent international nongovernment organization with a robust cross-border development program in this border region. AKDN's cross-border program is based on the integrated and area development approach—targeting the most isolated areas and vulnerable communities in northern Afghanistan and its respective cross-border areas. The program[25] has evolved since the completion of the first cross-border bridge in 2006, which linked Shugnan district of Afghanistan with Khorog town in Tajikistan. Over 10 years, AKDN, in collaboration with both governments, constructed four more bridges as part of its commitment to increase regional stability and prosperity in Gorno–Badakhshan of Tajikistan and Badakhshan province of Afghanistan. The cross-border bridges have provided Afghans access to the cross-border markets and "critical social services such as emergency medical treatment at Tajikistan hospitals and created more efficient delivery channels for humanitarian aid in once remote areas."[26] With the increasing number[27] of people using the bridges, relations between people from the two countries have strengthened and communities have benefited from the exchange of knowledge and experiences.

(iii.) Azerbaijan and Georgia Border

45.   Azerbaijan and Georgia share 480 km of borders. They are strategic partners, extending their successful cooperation to trade and investment, energy, transport, banking and finance, agriculture, sport, education, and culture.[28] Development in border regions between these countries is significantly different from the rest of the CAREC region, as the bordering areas are relatively well developed due to higher income levels and economic integration between them.

---

[22]   Funded by the EU, Border Management in Northern Afghanistan supports cross-border security and cooperation. It assists the Government of Afghanistan to increase economic and political relations between Afghanistan and the rest of the countries in the region by promoting economic development and stability. See UNDP. Border Management in Northern Afghanistan II (BOMNAF II).

[23]   Launched in 2014 with financial support from the Government of Japan, Livelihood Improvement in Tajik–Afghan Cross-Border Areas (LITACA) was initially a 3-year initiative to promote stability and security in the targeted communities in Tajikistan and Afghanistan in partnership with the relevant line ministries. The second phase, LITACA II (2018–2020), also with financial support from Japan, aims at increasing local governments' capacity, building basic infrastructure, and promoting economic activities in 12 bordering provinces and districts between Afghanistan and Tajikistan.

[24]   Aga Khan Development Network.

[25]   C. Wilton-Steer. 2018. Reconnecting Afghan & Tajik Badakhshan: Economic Development in the Cross-Border Region. Aga Khan Foundation UK. *Aga Khan Foundation UK*. 19. December.

[26]   Footnote 25. As the region is highly prone to natural disasters, including floods, landslides, and earthquake, delivery of emergency relief services to the Afghan Badakhshan is much easier than Tajik Badakhshan due to the short distance.

[27]   Based on the figures provided by the Tajik Border Security Forces at Darwaz cross-border market, 400–500 Afghans cross the bridge to visit the market every Saturday.

[28]   The Georgian Chamber of Commerce and Industry in Tbilisi informed the ADB field mission that Georgian information technology firms are looking to expand to Baku, Azerbaijan as their market provides expansion opportunities, and that Tbilisi-based retailers and medical service providers cater to Azerbaijani customers.

46.   The border community is predominantly rural, except for Kvemo Kartli, Georgia, where urbanization is about 40%. In the Sheki-Zagatala economic region in Azerbaijan, 27.6% of the population live in cities, while 72.4% is rural. In the Ganja-Gazakh region in Azerbaijan, 46.3% of the population live in towns, and 53.7% are rural.[29] About 500,000 ethnic Azerbaijanis live in the border areas of Georgia and Azerbaijan.[30] A liberalized, reciprocal visa regime supports the cross-border movement of border communities. The inhabitants of the city of Marneuli in Kvemo Kartli—Georgian region bordering with Azerbaijan—are ethnic Azerbaijanis and often hold dual passports. Ethnic Azerbaijani communities in Georgia find integration in Georgian society difficult due to increasing language and communication barriers. This could potentially lead to further marginalization of Azeri women.[31]

47.   Border communities in the Azerbaijani side often cross to the Georgian side to buy various products and avail of private health services. The border region between Lagodekhi (Georgia) and Balakan (Azerbaijan) provides a good example of successful cross-border cooperation, as the local municipalities jointly organize cultural and sports events.

48.   **Tourism** has increased between these two countries. Bordering regions—such as Kakheti and Kvemo Kartli in Georgia, and Ganja, Sheki, and Gabala in Azerbaijan—offer good conditions for the joint development of touristic products (footnote 7). This border region has numerous ancient cultural monuments, some of them original from the Stone Age, and in natural sites, from thermal springs to mountain peaks. Joint tourism products have been developed by initiatives such as the Eastern Partnership Territorial Cooperation (EAPTC) Program[32] (Box 3).

Box 3: Cross-Border Tourist Route between Azerbaijan and Georgia

The Eastern Partnership Territorial Cooperation project Civil Society for Development and Cooperation: Increasing Tourism Potential in the Bordering Regions of Azerbaijan and Georgia allowed Koda Community Education Center in Kvemo Kartli region (Georgia) and Ganja Regional Women's Centre Public Union in Ganja-Gazakh region (Azerbaijan), among other achievements, to jointly develop five tourist routes, two of which were cross-border between Azerbaijan and Georgia. These routes let the tourist discover the German heritage in these bordering regions and other cultural sites.

Sources: Koda Community Education Center; and Megoturi. About us.

49.   **Agriculture** also plays a dominant role in border communities' development in regions such as Sheki-Gabala in Azerbaijan, and Kakheti in Georgia. In these regions, viticulture, growing grapes, and winemaking have historical roots, and related products are widely exported, also offering opportunities to develop joint initiatives for border communities' development.

---

[29]   Eastern Partnership Territorial Cooperation Support Programme, Azerbaijan–Georgia Joint Operational Programme. p. 5

[30]   I. Hasanli. 2018. *Country Report: Azerbaijan Borders.* Centre for National and International Studies.

[31]   The Union of the Azerbaijan Women of Georgia, a nonprofit, nongovernment organization in Marneuli, Kvemo Kartli, promotes the association of the Azerbaijani women of Georgia for the protection of their rights and supports democratic reforms and civil society in Georgia.

[32]   Deutsche Gesellschaft für Internationale Zusammenarbeit (GIZ). Eastern Partnership Territorial Cooperation within the Context of the Local Governance Programme South Caucasus.

50.   The close ties between the two countries were further strengthened by the EU's Eastern Partnership Territorial Cooperation (EAPTC) program, which aimed at (i) empowering young people living in cross-border regions by increasing their employability skills through training and communication between potential employers and beneficiaries, (ii) increasing tourism potential in bordering regions, (iii) improving agricultural pest control in bordering areas, and (iv) facilitating the integration of children with disabilities living in border regions through joint training courses and awareness campaigns.

51.   The EU-funded **Red Bridge Project**[33] also proved to be a transformative cross-border infrastructure project, supporting the Azerbaijan and Georgia governments in securing their borders and facilitating the legal passage of persons and goods between the Ganja-Gazakh region (Azerbaijan) and Mughanlo village in Kvemo Kartli region (Georgia).

(iv.) People's Republic of China and Mongolia Border

52.   Mongolia borders to the south with two autonomous regions of the PRC—Xinjiang Uygur Autonomous Region and Inner Mongolia Autonomous Region—sharing 4,600 km of borders. The western end is marked by the Altai Mountains in Xinjiang, and the Gobi Desert is part of the eastern end of the border. Inner Mongolia has a sizable Mongol population of over 4 million, the largest Mongolian population in the world (bigger than Mongolia).[34]

53.   The PRC and Mongolia are **strategic trade partners**,[35] accounting for a bilateral cross-border trade volume of more than 70% through one of the main crossing points between the two countries: one between Erenhot, Inner Mongolia Autonomous Region in the PRC, and Zamyn-Uud in Mongolia.[36]

54.   The **Erenhot–Zamyn-Uud Cross-Border Economic Cooperation Zone**[37] is in this border crossing point. It deepens trade cooperation between the two countries and contributes to border communities' development with a duty-free trading facility where border communities can rent shop spaces to sell local products for 5% of their monthly business revenue. The free trade agreement between the PRC and Mongolia, currently under negotiation, will facilitate and strengthen this bilateral cooperation. In Inner Mongolia, the border city of Ulanqab is a trade node for commodities from the PRC, such as light industry products, fruits, and vegetables, which are later exported to Mongolia, the Russian Federation, and Europe through China Railway Express services. Minerals and timber from the Russian Federation and Mongolia are exported to the PRC through the returning trains.[38] This economic activity also contributes to the border communities' development.

---

[33]   The Red Bridge Project aimed at improving phytosanitary and veterinary control standards on this crossing point. To do that, capacity building programs to the staff of the crossing point were conducted. In addition, physical infrastructure was developed, and necessary equipment was provided to both sides of the border. For example, a secured customs area was built in Azerbaijan and control facilities were developed in Georgia. See UNDP. Development of Red Bridge Border Crossing Point between Georgia and Azerbaijan.

[34]   R. Zhou. 2019. The Mongol Minority. *China Highlights*. 17 January.

[35]   *China Daily*. 2014. China, Mongolia Upgrade Ties to Comprehensive Strategic Partnership. Mongolia and the PRC upgraded in 2014 their bilateral relations to a strategic partnership that set specific priority areas to expand and secure their economic cooperation, such as natural resources, infrastructure, and increased center-driven state-to-state political communication.

[36]   In 2019, the trade volume between the PRC and Mongolia reached $8.9 billion, which accounted for 64.4% of total foreign trade of Mongolia. *Xinhuanet*. 2020. Mongolia-China Trade Volume Reaches 8.9 Bln USD in 2019. 26 January.

[37]   In 2015, the PRC and Mongolia agreed that 9 square km on each side of their borders would be dedicated for the development of a joint economic zone. This economic zone would comprise territory in Erenhot (Inner Mongolia Autonomous Region, PRC) and Zamyn-Uud (Mongolia).

[38]   *CGTN*. 2018. Retracking the Ancient Silk Road: Ulanqab: New Future for the Old Caravansaries. 4 October.

55.	In terms of **people mobility**, Mongolian citizens can travel to the PRC for 30 days visa-free. Thus, Mongolian border communities can move freely and buy wholesale goods in the PRC for their respective local markets. Inner Mongolia Autonomous Region in the PRC offers Mongolians employment opportunities, mostly in industries such as media, sports, and arts. Visa for Chinese entering Mongolia is still required prior to travel.

56.	**Tourism** plays a pivotal role in the trilateral cooperation between the PRC, Mongolia, and the Russian Federation. In 2016, these countries established the **Tea Road International Tourism Alliance** due to the growing appeal of the Russian Federation and Mongolia as tourist destinations for Chinese travelers.[39] Under this alliance, a wide range of related travel products have been jointly developed, such as an international self-driving tour, a special train, and a summer camp.[40] In June 2019, the **Tea Road Cultural Tourism Expo** was held in Ulaanqab, Inner Mongolia Autonomous Region in the PRC, aiming to showcase the history and culture of the Tea Road and the unique local cultures, tourism landscapes, cultural and creative products, intangible cultural heritage items, and cross-border tourism routes.[41] This increase in tourism is envisioned to greatly impact livelihood opportunities for communities involved and boost the intensive development of other related industries such as transport, catering, and entertainment.

57.	The Erenhot local government in Inner Mongolia Autonomous Region in the PRC also supports residents of the East Gobi province of Mongolia that are seeking **medical care** in the PRC, giving them a 20% discount on medicines and medical treatment. Under this initiative, approximately 2,000–3,000 Mongolians from the East Gobi province benefit from medical treatment in Erenhot annually. In the absence of such initiatives, Mongolian border communities would have to make a trip of 3,000 km to the capital, Ulaanbaatar, to seek medical care.

## (v.)	Fergana Valley: Kyrgyz Republic, Tajikistan, and Uzbekistan

58.	The Fergana Valley encompasses an area in three countries—the Kyrgyz Republic, Tajikistan, and Uzbekistan. The Kyrgyz Republic shares 984 km with Tajikistan and 1,314 km with Uzbekistan, while Tajikistan has 1,312 km of common borders with Uzbekistan. The Fergana Valley crisscrosses these three countries, bringing together communities from part of the Kyrgyz oblasts of Batken, Jalal-Abad, and Osh; part of Soghd Region in Tajikistan; and Andijan, Fergana, Kokand, and Namangan in Uzbekistan.

59.	It is an ethnically complex region, consisting mainly of Kyrgyz, Tajiks, and Uzbeks. Almost a quarter of the five Central Asian countries' (Kazakhstan, the Kyrgyz Republic, Tajikistan, Turkmenistan, and Uzbekistan) population live in the Fergana Valley, attracted by the favorable conditions for agriculture of the area. "With a total population estimated at 14 million across all three countries, the portion of Fergana Valley located in Uzbekistan is the largest, with approximately 9.3 million people, comprising 28% of Uzbekistan's total population"[42]—the largest stakeholder in the valley in terms of territory and population.

60.	Recent developments and increased cooperation between these countries have improved connectivity between bordering regions and people interaction. For example, in 2018, Uzbekistan and

---

39	In 2018, more than 2.4 million Russian tourists visited the PRC, a 3% year-on-year increase. The number of visitors from Mongolia to the PRC rose 2.8% to more than 1.9 million. Nearly 200,000 Chinese visitors were received by Mongolia, a 19% growth. *Russia Business Today.* 2019. Russia to Boost Tourism Links to China, Mongolia. 24 June.

40	H. Zhe. 2019. China, Russia, and Mongolia Meet to Reinforce Trilateral Tourism Ties. *China Daily.* 24 June.

41	*China Daily.* 2019. Tea Road Cultural Tourism Expo Opens in Ulaanqab. 24 June.

42	World Bank. 2018. *Project information Document/ Integrated Safeguards Data Sheet: Uzbekistan Prosperous Villages.* 10 September. p. 9.

Tajikistan signed a strategic partnership agreement and opened more than 10 new **border crossing points**. Similarly, Uzbekistan and the Kyrgyz Republic are negotiating border demarcation peacefully, and progress is being made on the construction of a railway line that can further increase connectivity between them and the PRC. The movement of people between these three countries is allowed **visa-free**.

61.　　Cross-border interaction between border community members happens through formal and informal trading (Box 4). **Kara-Suu market of Osh region** is one of the largest markets in the Kyrgyz Republic and the Fergana Valley and is a successful practice of promoting border communities' mobility.[43] After the launch of the major border checkpoint—Dostuk—between the Kyrgyz Republic and Uzbekistan, the number of customers from Uzbekistan going to the market increased. The market itself was replenished with agricultural products from the bordering areas, although most goods come from the PRC.

Box 4: Informal Economy in the Kyrgyz Republic–Tajikistan and Kyrgyz Republic–Uzbekistan Borders

Elmira lives in Batken, a village in the border between the Kyrgyz Republic and Tajikistan. She regularly crosses the border to the Tajikistan side to buy cheap household goods and then sells them in the market on the Kyrgyz Republic side for a higher price. Smuggling small amounts of goods and produce is a common practice by many other residents in bordering regions like Elmira. They avoid the customs regime established after both countries became members of the Eurasian Economic Union in 2015.

The Dostuk area, in the border between Osh, Kyrgyz Republic, and Uzbekistan, is also a place where small smuggling practices can be observed. Salt is often smuggled from Uzbekistan into the Kyrgyz Republic by men on bicycles, while women enter aluminum into the country.

Source: D. Mamatova. 2018. The Central Asian Valley where Borders Dissolve in Grassroots Cooperation. *OpenDemocracy.* 7 December.

62.　　The **Ferghana Valley Rural Enterprise Development Project**[44] supports micro, small, and medium-sized enterprises (MSMEs) in rural border areas of the Fergana Valley. It aims to strengthen linkages in supply chains and facilitate greater access to markets in rural border areas such as Andijan, Fergana, and Namangan in Uzbekistan.

63.　　The common use of water and pastures also contributes to building trust between communities, improving relationships, and forging cross-border networks. However, **water scarcity and ineffective water governance** still cause occasional conflicts between border communities in the valley. The irrigation canals network across the Fergana Valley is extremely complex. Overuse of water resources by upstream communities frequently limits water consumption by those downstream. To mitigate the risk, water user associations (WUAs) have been formed to manage water resources, operate irrigation and drainage infrastructure, and maintain former collective farming territories. Although international donors have taken an active role in the initial setup of the WUAs, additional support is still needed to develop them into effective organizations.[45] The expected 35%–40% population growth by 2050 places enormous pressure on the already scarce resources in the region and heightens the competition for jobs. Securitization of

---

[43]　D. Umotbay uulu. 2018. A Day at the Largest Market of Fergana Valley. *Central Asian Bureau for Analytical Reporting.* 17 October.

[44]　World Bank. 2019. Ferghana Valley Rural Enterprise Development Project.

[45]　I. Abdullaev, J. Kazbekov, H. Manthrithilake, and K. Jumaboev. 2009. Water User Groups in Central Asia: Emerging Form of Collective Action in Irrigation Water Management. *Water Resources Management.* 24 (5). pp. 1029–1043.

borders also causes sporadic conflicts between border communities in the valley.[46] However, securitization is overcome through everyday cooperation, like in the Ferghana Valley (Box 5).

Box 5: Shared Use of Water and Pasture in the Kyrgyz Republic–Tajikistan Border

Water user associations (WUA) administer the different hydrographic zones in the Ferghana Valley. Myrza-Patcha is a village in the Isfana district of Batken province, Kyrgyz Republic. However, this village is not included in WUA's corresponding hydrographic zone. The Isfana River runs along the Kyrgyz-Tajik border, and is a major source of water for communities living on both sides of the border. In the event of mudslides, neighboring communities organize "ashar" (collective labor) to clean the riverbed.

Residents living along this border also share pastures. Unofficial arrangements are set between Kyrgyz and Tajik dwellers, heads of pasture committees, and heads of villages for Tajik villagers to feed their cattle in the pastures of Myrza-Patcha.

Source: D. Mamatova. 2018. The Central Asian Valley where Borders Dissolve in Grassroots Cooperation. *OpenDemocracy*. 7 December.

3.3 Key Findings from Analysis of CAREC Borders

64. Cross-border communities living in the border areas described above vary greatly due to the CAREC region's diversity. They are influenced by their history and the current state of affairs between countries. However, it is possible to identify the following common factors for designing and implementing potential initiatives to promote people-to-people connectivity and border communities' development:

(i) Cross-border cooperation can significantly improve border communities' livelihood opportunities and increase their access to social services.

(ii) Institutional efforts to create an enabling environment for cross-border cooperation and people-to-people contacts are often limited. Successful initiatives involve fully engaged local administrative bodies that are supported by national policy framework and institutions.

(iii) Where regulations on people mobility, such as visa regimes or border crossing points, are friendly, cross-border initiatives are more effective.

(iv) Successful community collaboration programs have been implemented along and across CAREC borders and involve a wide range of sectors, from enhancing trading activities to tourism, from educational exchanges to improved access to necessary amenities such as health care.

(v) Existing initiatives need to be scaled up and made more sustainable.

(vi) Vulnerable groups in border communities, such as youth, women and girls, children, and the elderly, face specific challenges. Therefore, initiatives need to be designed correspondingly for targeted beneficiaries.

(vii) Climate change exposes the border regions' population to disproportionate impacts owing to their cultural and institutional diversity and uneven economic development.

(viii) Several programs and organizations implement initiatives to promote people-to-people contacts and develop border communities with local expertise. CAREC could also seek partnerships with AKDN, the EU, PATRIP, and UNDP, among others.

---

[46] University of Central Asia. 2019. Kyrgyz Republic: Current Dynamics of the Border Areas in the Fergana Valley Workshop. 14 February.

65.   To build upon these findings, the team analyzed experiences from international institutions to promote cross-border community collaboration. Experiences show that successful cross-border cooperation happens where regional, national, and local participants, including governments, local associations, and civil society organizations (CSOs), are effectively engaged and assume responsibility. Strengthening regional and local bodies is the most appropriate mechanism at the administrative level for effective cross-border cooperation, which would increase their authority and flexibility to provide needed support to cross-border communities to ensure that structures on both sides of the border have balanced competencies.[47]

66.   From a global and historical perspective, CAREC countries are not unique in their desire to create a more unified region and community. Diverse regions have achieved success while dealing with challenges not different from those faced by CAREC countries today, as shown in the **European Union (EU)**, the **Nordic European region**, the **Association of Southeast Asian Nations (ASEAN)**, and the **African Union**[48] **(AU)**. These cases provide useful analogies and examples of cross-border cooperation against the background of diverse economic and cultural environments of their constituent members.

4.1. European Union

67.   In the 1950s, after the Second World War, representatives of several European border areas discussed ways to ease restrictions of border barriers and explored possibilities for cross-border cooperation to increase the living standards of cross-border communities, guarantee a peaceful environment, and ease border restrictions and other factors. The construction of bridges and tunnels also contributed to overcome natural borders. To improve cross-border cooperation, European countries established local and regional associations on both sides of the border. For example, the **Association of European Border Regions** was founded in 1971, creating bonds with other European institutions, such as the Council of Europe, the European Parliament, the European Commission, and countries' governments.[49]

68.   The network of the border and cross-border regions in Europe has been a driving force behind the EU. To eliminate problems in border regions and achieve sustainable cross-border integration, the Council of Europe developed in the 1980s specific agreements, treaties, legal forms and models for the harmonization of many areas of law.[50] These were supported by national governments and enabled the

---

[47] M. Slusarciuc. 2013. Partnership and Cooperation Models in Cross-Border Areas. *AUDŒ*. 9 (4). pp. 267–280.

[48] The AU is a continental body consisting of 55 member states that make up the countries on the African continent. It was officially launched in 2002 as a successor to the Organization of African Unity (1963–1999). See African Union.

[49] N. Kakubava and T. Chincharauli. 2010. *Cross-Border Cooperation: Practical Guide.* Association of Young Economists of Georgia.

[50] E. Medeiros. 2018. *European Territorial Cooperation: Theoretical and Empirical Approaches to the Process and Impacts of Cross-Border and Transnational Cooperation in Europe.* Springer International Publishing.

development of joint cross-border programs. For economic cooperation activities, for example, specific instruments of European law are used, such as the European Economic Interest Grouping, or the Public Interest Grouping and Mixed Economy Company.

69.   Since internal borders of the EU were dismantled, common external borders needed to be secured to grant a progressive development of the region. To fund cross-border cooperation, the European Union has used different sources of funding, such as the European Regional Development Fund. After the expansion of the EU in 2004 and the establishment of the Schengen area[51] in 2007, a new visa regime was introduced, which regularized the flow of goods and people across the EU's external borders. Border regions' major source of income and development had been until then unofficial small-scale trading activities. Accession to the EU required the harmonization of border controls and the adoption of the common visa regime and customs rules, which threatened the fragile ecosystem of the border communities living of undeclared trading practices.

70.   A lesson the CAREC Program can draw from the EU external border development is that establishing associations at local and regional levels on both sides of the border can improve cross-border cooperation. Modeled along the EU's Schengen visa agreement is the proposed Silk Road visa, which "would permit all countries located along the Silk Road to be visited on a single tourist visa."[52] This initiative would also have implications on the border management of CAREC member countries that share land borders with the Silk Road visa countries.

4.2. Nordic European Region

71.   The **Nordic European region**, comprising Denmark, Finland, Iceland, Norway, and Sweden, share a close cultural, religious, and historical background, similar to the relationship among the CAREC member countries. Scandinavian languages, like Turkic languages in some of the CAREC countries, are closely related. Finnish, like Tajik, is of a different origin. Besides, the Nordic European countries are also members of different cooperation organizations.

72.   The Nordic model demonstrates that different approaches to cooperation do not need to be an obstacle for regional cooperation and integration. It also shows that it is possible to develop effective regional cooperation mechanisms and that different approaches can be complementary. As of today, the Nordic cooperation allows Norway to stay informed about EU issues, and Sweden and Finland about the North Atlantic Treaty Organization.[53]

---

[51] "Schengen area signifies a zone where 26 European countries abolished their internal borders for the free and unrestricted movement of people, in harmony with common rules for controlling external borders and fighting criminality." SchengenVisaInfo.com. Schengen Area – The World's Largest Visa Free Zone.

[52] Footnote 7, p. 21.

[53] S. E. Cornell and S. F. Starr. 2018. Regional Cooperation in Central Asia: Relevance of World Models. *The Central Asia-Caucasus Analyst.* 4 December.

4.3. Association of Southeast Asian Nations

73.   Like the CAREC countries, **ASEAN member states**[54] speak different languages, are comprised of several ethnicities, profess diverse religions, and show uneven economic development. **ASEAN** was formed in 1967 and has proved itself since then as an effective association, focusing on strengthening their institutional structures. CAREC could follow this example to support cross-border communities locally by strengthening corresponding local bodies. The work of the local bodies is, of course, most effective when supported by the corresponding priorities at national and international top levels.

4.4. African Union

74.   There are multiple **regional unions in Africa**, similar to the CAREC region.[55] These unions gather people from the same geographic zone to get involved in trading and business activities. Over the years, they have established arrangements to support integration at different dimensions—economic, trade facilitation, and transportation—promoting people-to-people connectivity across borders and border communities' development. With this aim, legal instruments have been put in place to institutionalize some of these regional unions' functions.

75.   While the success of some of these unions comes from their independence of formal institutions, progressive and selected institutional partnerships also increase their scope, scale, and sustainability. Thus, the AU acts as an administrative tool to oversee and direct these community bodies in consolidating their roles and operations.[56]

---

[54] ASEAN has 10 members: Brunei Darussalam, Cambodia, Indonesia, the Lao People's Democratic Republic, Malaysia, Myanmar, the Philippines, Singapore, Thailand, and Viet Nam.

[55] These unions include the "West African Economic and Monetary Union within the ambit of the Economic Community of West African States and the Economic and Monetary Union of Central Africa within the Economic Community of Central African States region. Within the geographic area of Common Market for Eastern and Southern Africa there are the Southern African Customs Union with its associated monetary union (the Common Monetary Area), the Southern African Development Community and the East African Community. Some countries in this region are also joined with countries in the Horn of Africa in the Intergovernmental Authority on Development". A. Matthews. 2003. Regional Integration in Africa. In *Regional Integration and Food Security in Developing Countries*. Food and Agriculture Organization of the United Nations. Rome.

[56] I. Chirisa, O. S. Dirwai, and A. Mumba. 2014. A Review of the Evolution and Trajectory of the African Union as an Instrument of Regional Integration. *SpringerPlus*. 2014 (3). pp. 101–114.

5. Strengths, Weaknesses, Opportunities, and Threats Analysis

76.　　　Despite progress, the scope for expanding cross-community collaboration in the border areas remains very large, particularly if some of the identified physical barriers and policy and regulatory bottlenecks can be addressed. To set the stage for the recommendations, the team summarized a brief strengths, weaknesses, opportunities, and threats (SWOT) analysis of the scope for CAREC to strengthen cross-border communities' development (Table 2).

Table 2: Strengths, Weaknesses, Opportunities, and Threats Analysis

Strengths	Weaknesses
• The CAREC Program is a well-established regional cooperation platform with active engagement with national governments. • CAREC 2030 envisages focusing on investments in and policy dialogue on five operational clusters, including some sectors with great potential to promote people-to-people contacts and border communities' development, such as connectivity, trade, education, tourism, health, and agriculture. • Despite their differences, border communities in the CAREC region often share traditional cultural, linguistic, and economic ties that lay the groundwork for integrated initiatives.	• CAREC activities for cross-border community development can be hindered by the peripheral status of border regions with no major policy influence in capitals. • Development initiatives could be overwhelming due to high unemployment rates in border areas. • Public service delivery is weak in the border regions in several sectors such as education and health care. • People mobility is limited due to limited infrastructure, visa restrictions, security environment, and incompatible legal and administrative systems across borders. • Coordination and information sharing by border management agencies in trade and customs rules are insufficient. • Cross-border institutions are limited to ensure strategic and effective cross-border movement of goods and people, and to create an enabling environment for greater cross-border cooperation. • State-to-state relations vary across the region. • Patriarchal sociocultural practices hinder women from full participation in economic activities in border areas.

continued on next page

Table 2 *continued*

Opportunities	Threats
• Existing cross-border infrastructure networks and projects could be used by CAREC to boost border communities' development.	• Climate change effects will be experienced, particularly on border areas prone to natural disasters such as floods.
• Information and communication technology is speeding up processes in border crossing points and allowing e-commerce and could be increased with CAREC support for border communities' development.	• Competition over natural resources may cause conflicts between bordering communities.
• Formal and informal trade networks across borders could be further utilized by CAREC to promote trade initiatives.	• Pandemics, such as the recent COVID-19, directly conflict with social integration and cause borders lockdown.
• The regional trend toward easing visa regulations could facilitate border community contacts and allow increased travel and transit between CAREC countries.	• Political instability in many regions and broader security issues also pose a major threat.
• The region's rich cultural heritage offers potential for cross-border tourism, which CAREC can help develop.	
• Examples of economic cooperation zones projects in the region could be expanded to boost related industrial development in border areas.	
• Potential CAREC support to local micro, small, and medium-sized enterprises in border areas could increase economic opportunities.	
• CAREC could partner with other institutions interested in supporting cross-border community development.	
• Ongoing studies by CAREC on several sectors, such as education, tourism, health, and agriculture, offer an important modality to propose and adapt recommendations for border communities' development.	

CAREC = Central Asia Regional Economic Cooperation, COVID-19 = coronavirus disease.
Source: CAREC Secretariat.

77.   The following sections 5.1 and 5.2 strengthen the context and provide a strategic framework to underpin recommendations proposed in section 6.

5.1. Building on Strengths and Capturing Opportunities

78.   Given the strengths of CAREC as a regional cooperation platform—the border communities shared ties and existing beneficial external factors such as favorable foreign policies and trends in the region, among other opportunities—some strategies and initiatives can be pursued to promote people-to-people contacts and develop cross-border communities in the region.

(i.) Leverage Positive Regional Trends

79. Reforms in Uzbekistan's development since 2016 have had a positive effect on the prospects of regional cooperation in the rest of CAREC countries. Uzbekistan's new action strategy for 2017–2021, with foreign policy on strengthening ties with neighboring countries, will ensure shared future prosperity and development for the whole region. Furthermore, the Eurasian Economic Union guarantees the free movement of goods, capital, services, and people; and develops common policies in different sectors such as economy, transport, industry and agriculture, energy, foreign trade and investment, customs, and technical regulation.[57]

80. In addition, since 2017, countries such as Kazakhstan, the Kyrgyz Republic, Uzbekistan, and Tajikistan have liberalized their entry policies. Kazakhstan and Uzbekistan have proposed a Schengen-type visa arrangement. Azerbaijan and Georgia have liberalized their visa regime on reciprocity bases. Mongolian citizens can travel to the PRC for 30 days visa-free. Policies like these, support border community development.

81. CAREC should use this momentum to promote people mobility in the region through initiatives that build resilient and sustainable regional infrastructure, strengthen trade links, and create jobs and greater economic opportunities for all the member countries.

(ii.) Adopt a Community-Driven Approach

82. Given the importance of empowering communities in the bordering areas of the CAREC region, a community-driven development approach may be the most important component of a cross-border program to improve their living condition and promote people-to-people contacts. Through a community-driven development approach, both men and women residing on both sides of the border can find solutions to common problems.

83. Capacity building of grassroots institutions—including women's organizations, farmers' organizations, water user associations (WUAs), and pasture user committees—could serve as an effective platform to foster local development and cross-border cooperation. The regional and national governments would need to provide a legal framework to enable grassroots institutions to complement the local government's development work to plan, implement, and manage small infrastructure projects and improve the delivery of other public sector services.

(iii.) Build on Recommendations Provided by Other CAREC Studies

84. The CAREC Program focuses on investments in and policy dialogue on five operational clusters: (i) economic and financial stability; (ii) trade, tourism, and economic corridors; (iii) infrastructure and economic connectivity; (iv) agriculture and water; and (v) human development. In addition, gender equality, ICT integration, and climate change mitigation are cross-cutting themes across these five clusters. Some of these sectors, such as connectivity, trade, tourism, agriculture, education, and health, have great potential to promote people-to-people contacts and border community development. Activities being pursued by CAREC in these sectors and proposed initiatives in other scoping studies could be expanded and scaled up to achieve this goal.

---

[57] J. Chappelow. 2020. Eurasian Economic Union (EAEU). *Investopedia.* 18 September.

85.   **On tourism: develop community-based tourism.** As stated in the scoping study on promoting regional tourism cooperation under CAREC 2030, tourism can play an important role in spurring economic growth and promoting people's intra-regional movement for leisure and business in border communities. Community-based tourism should be promoted through product development, tourist information, human resources development, infrastructure development, as well as strengthening regional and subregional tourism associations and hosting tourism conferences along with sports and cultural festivals. Forming joint management structures on cross-border tourist sites promotes cross-border tourism and border communities' development in areas such as the Kura, Ganikh, and Gabirri transborder river on the Georgia–Azerbaijan border.

86.   **On education: enhance student and worker mobility.** Recommendations in the CAREC scoping study on education and skills development included harmonization of standards and strengthening mutual recognition of qualifications. Based on these recommendations, specific initiatives can be developed to promote student and worker mobility in CAREC border communities (footnote 4). These initiatives can include conducting events and virtual campaigns to raise the visibility of mobility programs among educational institutions in bordering countries, as well as providing technical and financial support for these institutions to participate in these programs.

87.   A **network of universities in the bordering regions**[58] or subregions could be formed for closer coordination in research and student exchange. The activities could include scholarships for graduate and postgraduate studies, with English as the instruction language, and academic conferences and workshops on common issues such as public policy, local economic development, energy, water, tourism, and development of mountain areas.

88.   Institutions such as the **University of Central Asia** or the **Nazarbayev University in Nur-Sultan, Kazakhstan** could play a leading role in attracting students from the CAREC region; providing continuing education in various professional areas, including community-led development approaches; and offering research opportunities to young professionals from the CAREC region.

89.   **Strengthen labor–market information and labor movement.** As highlighted in the CAREC scoping study on education and skills development, some CAREC countries, such as the Kyrgyz Republic, Pakistan, Tajikistan, and Uzbekistan, "are major exporters of labor and are highly reliant on migrant workers' remittances for foreign exchange and employment."[59] "One of the challenges facing CAREC countries is the mismatch between skills demand and supply, and this is often due to the limited availability of systematic information on labor–market needs" (footnote 59). The CAREC scoping study on education recommends that a regional labor–market information system be established to facilitate the planning of labor–market and technical and vocational education policies in both the sending and receiving countries. This initiative would be particularly beneficial for bordering countries, which suffer from high unemployment rates, with some citizens often crossing the border to seek job opportunities.

90.   **On health.** The main purpose of cross-border collaboration for health is to ensure sustainable improvements in the health status of communities by pooling scarce resources and providing access. It is necessary to work closely with communities and encourage them to take responsibility for their own

---

[58]   Khorog (Tajikistan), Osh (Kyrgyz Republic), Tashkent (Uzbekistan), Almaty (Kazakhstan), Faizabad (Afghanistan), Kashgar (Xinjiang Uygur Autonomous Region, PRC), Peshawar (Pakistan), Turkmenabad (Turkmenistan), and Bukhara (Uzbekistan).

[59]   Footnote 4, p. 33.

health.[60] Building on the ongoing work of formulating a CAREC scoping study on regional health, the team proposed the following two guidelines.

91.　　**Developing a cross-border health cooperation plan.** Plans between neighboring countries can consider opening regional health-care facilities linked to district health facilities across the border through e-health systems. Primary health-care services can be enhanced through a family medicine model. Access to health-care services can be improved through community-based health financing schemes.

92.　　**Strengthening secondary and tertiary health-care services** and opening them for the cross-border population can also be considered to support activities on human development, such as providing capacity building for government health professionals and facilitating networking.

(iv.) Develop Agriculture and Livestock Value Chains

93.　　Agriculture is a major source of livelihood for people living along the CAREC borders. Development of agriculture and livestock value chains should be supported under cross-border programs, which can include (i) capacity building, (ii) events for knowledge sharing, and (iii) promotion of regional organizations.

94.　　**On capacity building, farmers can be trained** in crop and livestock production, adaptation to climate change and mitigation, plant protection, disease control, and postharvest technologies. Support can also be provided to processors in areas like phytosanitary and animal measures to meet international quality standards. This capacity building can be extended to WUAs and growers' and marketing associations providing services to border communities.

95.　　**Knowledge sharing, regional investment conferences, trade fairs, and farmers' forums** can be conducted to share knowledge and experiences among farmers from bordering areas to find solutions to common problems related to access to agriculture and livestock markets, irrigation, climate change effects, land erosion, and conservation. Chambers of commerce support can be sought.

96.　　**To promote regional organizations, regional farmers' organizations** can be established to help farmers from bordering areas build social capital and provide a platform for their interaction with other farmers across the border.

(v.) Strengthen Role of the Private Sector and Civil Society

97.　　In the CAREC context, the private sector can play a major role in developing border communities and enhancing people-to-people contacts across borders, and as stakeholder, partner, and service provider for border agencies. For example, in border management initiatives, private sector involvement can benefit border agencies through consultation, collaboration, and contracting. Some initiatives aiming at this goal are explained above. Additional activities that could be pursued are the following.

98.　　**A regional chamber of commerce working group** can be created to support chambers of commerce to promote business-to-business contacts, whose research and policy notes can be disseminated by the CAREC Institute and used as political advocacy tools among member states to promote pro-commerce policies in the CAREC region.

---

[60]　Through health awareness sessions and sensitization, people can be motivated to take responsibility of their own health.

99.   **Trade facilitation centers**[61] can be established at the existing cross-border markets to exchange information on trade policies, custom duties, investment, and trading opportunities to promote free movement of traders, businesspersons, capital, goods, and services across the borders.

100.   **Cross-border business forums** can be conducted to identify administrative and legal barriers, reform trade policies, develop links with financial institutions, facilitate joint ventures, and share experiences and lessons from small business operations.

101.   **Joint training for entrepreneurs in business planning and management** can help potential entrepreneurs on both sides of the border develop personal relations, which may transpire into joint business ventures. Setting up venture capital funds may also be considered to finance business start-ups and provide working capital to existing businesses.

102.   The **civil society organizations (CSOs)** represent the interest of their members. Therefore, their capacity should be strengthened to further engage with the public and the private sectors for project implementation and to improve governance and accountability. Capacity building can be conducted through training and networking, exposure visits, and knowledge sharing. Arranging local and regional civil society forums can be considered for regional cross-border programs.

103.   A regional **CAREC civil society forum** would be an important institutional platform to promote interaction between the CSOs of the member countries for knowledge sharing. It can be steered along with other partners such as the Aga Khan Development Network (AKDN), the Deutsche Gesellschaft für Internationale Zusammenarbeit (GIZ) program, the EU, and the United Nations Development Programme (UNDP). Participating CSOs can include youth associations, teachers' associations, and women's organizations.

104.   **Regional tour operators' association, regional cultural forum, CAREC universities network forum**, and **CAREC youth forum** are other forms of social organization.

5.2. Addressing Weaknesses and Challenges

105.   High priority has been traditionally given to measures that upgrade infrastructure and communications in the region to overcome the natural geographic barriers between CAREC countries, improve the peripheral status of border communities, and remove the transit obstacles within the CAREC region. However, further support should also be given to initiatives that specifically develop border communities, such as those explained below.

(i.)   Promote Border and Cross-Border Markets in Border Regions

106.   Border regions in peripheral areas in the CAREC member countries are regarded as least-developed rural regions. They have high unemployment, low wages, and limited opportunities for formal employment. Participation in the informal economy is often the primary source of income for border

---

[61]   The Balochistan Rural Support Programme and Sarhad Rural Support Programme have established trade facilitation centers in the Pakistan–Afghanistan border in the Khyber Pass and Balochistan provinces, which facilitate traders and businesspeople from both sides of the border.

communities. Public service delivery is weak. Border and cross-border markets can facilitate greater interaction between communities across borders and promote subregional MSMEs.[62]

(ii.) Increase Participation of Micro, Small, and Medium-Sized Enterprises

107.   The need and potential for MSMEs development in cross-border regions are different for each region, depending on the level of development, patterns of contact, and trade dynamics across the border, including administrative and regulatory barriers. Tailored actions can be developed to support MSMEs in the borders, including informative and advisory sessions, general and specific trainings, and provision of physical facilities such as business incubators and exhibition spaces.

108.   Innovation and technology can strengthen the MSMEs' competitiveness. Further support can be given to identify MSMEs' needs and problems in border regions and the necessary conditions to help them develop through ICT.[63]

(iii.) Address Impact of Climate Change in Border Communities

109.   Climate change has the potential to add pressure and constrain relations between CAREC member countries.[64] Projected climate change effects will challenge already deteriorated water systems and aggravate existing limited water supply and quality vulnerabilities in CAREC border regions. Embedded effects of this additional stress may include challenges to energy infrastructure, agriculture, food security, and traditional farming. "In the absence of mutual trust and functional resource sharing arrangements, desperation could aggravate historical disputes, inflate prejudice and misplace the blame," putting at risk the already vulnerable and marginalized communities in border regions (footnote 64).

110.   The CAREC Program can support a regional **climate change dialogue** and involve central and local governments, private sector, international organizations, and civil society. A cost-benefit analysis of cooperative frameworks for early warning and disaster relief can be conducted, which can ultimately help build a case to unlock political will (footnote 64). Citizens of certain CAREC border regions may be closer to a neighboring state's relief services. "However, transboundary early warning and disaster relief has not yet been established" (footnote 64).

(iv.) Strengthen Women's Role in Border Community Development

111.   Gender equality and women's empowerment are prerequisites for economic growth and inclusive, equitable, and sustainable development. Strengthening women's role and empowering them as active participants in border communities' development makes good economic sense, as it leads to reduced poverty, faster growth, and greater benefits for the whole society.

---

[62]   A model of controlled facilitation of informal economy is relevant today to the PRC–Pakistan, Pakistan–Afghanistan, Fergana Valley, and Afghanistan–Tajikistan border regions.

[63]   Under the Belt and Road Initiative, transnational digital and banking networks are being established and, therefore, can potentially facilitate information technology and financial services integration, enabling greater people-to-people contact. Memorandums of understanding on cooperation on the Digital Silk Road have been signed between the PRC and 16 countries, 11 Chinese banks have established 71 branches in 27 countries, and 41 countries are covered by the renminbi cross-border clearing system. *Xinhuanet.* 2019. Factbox: New Progress in Pursuit of Belt and Road Initiative. 19 March.

[64]   World Economic Forum. 2019. *Climate Change Is Threatening Security in Central Asia. Here Are Ways to Reduce the Risk.* 25 January.

112.   Therefore, CAREC, under the framework defined in the CAREC Gender Strategy 2030, can support initiatives aiming at strengthening women's role for border communities' development, in addition to national and regional efforts to achieve gender equality. Strategies paving the way for women in borders include support for the expansion of sectors with a large presence of women and address issues that impede the supply of female labor, such as gender-discriminatory regulations and laws, and limited women's access to essential services and assets, including education and trainings, networks, transportation infrastructure, credit, land, agricultural inputs, and ICTs. CAREC can also consider providing support to improve the prevention and detection of human trafficking, strengthen the protection and promotion of human rights, create more representative border management institutions, and enhance civil society oversight.[65] To define specific initiatives, CAREC can promote focus group discussion on different sectors (e.g., women traders) among women living in the borders to share their experiences as entrepreneurs.

---

[65]   A. Mackay. 2008. Border Management and Gender. In Megan Bastick and Kristin Valasek, eds. *Gender and Security Sector Reform Toolkit*. Geneva: DCAF, OSCE/ODIHR, UN-INSTRAW.

6. Recommendations for CAREC

113.   This study identifies a series of recommendations for CAREC to play a proactive role in expanding cross-border cooperation in border regions, based on lessons learned from international best practices and findings of the SWOT analysis. These recommendations can be implemented by adopting a community-driven approach and grouped into three categories:

(i)   **Sector-specific recommendations.** The proposed initiatives are related to specific sectors under the CAREC five operational clusters. It is recommended that planned CAREC initiatives pay attention to realizing the potential for regional cooperation through promoting cross-border community collaboration in these sectors and areas. An additional set of recommendations is provided on climate change as a crosscutting theme over the rest of the sectors.

(ii) **Institutional-level recommendations.** This set includes initiatives to strengthen local cross-border cooperation institutions' capacity.

(iii) **Gender equality recommendations.** In alignment with the CAREC Gender Strategy 2030, these initiatives aim to strengthen women's role in border community development.

114.   Proposed recommendations to pursue people-to-people connectivity and border community development in the CAREC region are summarized in Table 3.

Table 3: Summary of Recommendations for Border Community Development

A. Sector-Specific Recommendations	
Sector	**Recommendations**
Economic and financial sector	• Provide technical and financial support to MSMEs in the borders to create a conducive environment for promoting cross-border business through training and seeking partnerships with microfinance institutions and commercial banks.
Trade	• Support the establishment of trade facilitation centers in target areas. • Formulate diagnostic studies on the coordination mechanisms and protocols of border agencies to improve border management systems. • Create a regional chamber commerce working group to support chambers of commerce and promote business-to-business contacts. • Conduct cross-border business forums to strengthen the role of the private sector.
Tourism	• Establish a Regional Tour Operators' Association for knowledge exchange on promoting sustainable and community-based tourism in bordering regions. • Conduct a CAREC Tourism and Cultural Forum to facilitate networking and partnerships among public and private stakeholders, including from bordering areas.

continued on next page

Table 3 *continued*

A. Sector-Specific Recommendations

Sector	Recommendations
Agriculture	• Formulate a study on regional and cross-border agricultural value chains for agriculture in CAREC. • Strengthen policy and institutions for effective transboundary water management. • Train farmers on efficient water use and related technologies. • Conduct regional investment conferences, trade fairs, and farmers' forums to share knowledge and experiences, including participants from bordering areas. This could lead to establishing regional farmers' organizations.
Health	• Establish emergency health-care centers on selected border points to provide basic and emergency treatment to residents and border communities.
Education	• Conduct CAREC universities network forum and CAREC youth forum to empower the youth living in border regions. • Support cross-border programs for youth organizations, student exchanges, and joint research projects. Support technical and vocational training courses under cross-border programs.
Climate change	• Formulate a cost-benefit analysis of cooperative frameworks for early warning and disaster relief in bordering areas. • Conduct regional climate change dialogue with central and local governments, private sector, international organizations, and civil society, including border communities. • Provide training programs in clean energy, sustainable resource management, ecotourism, and energy-efficient technology promotion in border areas.

B. Institutional-Level Recommendations

- Formulate a scoping study on cross-border institutions and policies for border communities' development.
- Promote partnerships between CAREC and credible and bankable cross-border institutions.
- Support governments to develop legal frameworks to support cross-border programs.
- Support initiatives for raising awareness in central and regional governments about fostering enabling institutional frameworks for cross-border community development to promote successful public–private collaboration in this area.
- Provide capacity building and financing support for CSOs and private sector operating in border areas.
- Conduct CAREC civil society forum to promote interaction between people and CSOs of member countries, including from bordering areas.

C. Gender Equality Recommendations

- Formulate a study to take stock of grassroots institutions in the border regions that provide support to vulnerable groups such as women, youth, and people with special needs.
- Provide support to governments to develop gender-inclusive policies that ensure women living in bordering regions have access to decent work, economic opportunities, education and training, health services, ICT, infrastructure, and public services; and to participate in decision-making processes.
- Promote policy dialogue at regional and cross-country levels to enable stakeholders from across the region to learn from each other's experiences and put in place best practices for women's empowerment and gender mainstreaming in bordering regions.
- Conduct women forums and conferences to exchange knowledge on and best practices in different sectors such as trade. Facilitate networking between female entrepreneurs from bordering regions.
- Train border officials to minimize discrimination by gender in borders and strengthen the protection and promotion of human rights.

CAREC = Central Asia Regional Economic Cooperation, CSO = civil society organization, ICT = information and communication technology, MSMEs = micro, small, and medium-sized enterprises.

Source: CAREC Secretariat.

115.	ADB and other CAREC development partners could provide technical assistance as a start to facilitate dialogue and prepare robust project proposals to deepen community collaboration in the region. The CAREC Institute could also support undertaking research, training, and data dissemination relating to cross-border community collaboration.

116.	The impact of the recommendations above can promote people-to-people connectivity in the region and develop border communities, ultimately improving millions of people's lives and livelihoods for current and future generations. At the time of writing, the world is battling the COVID-19 pandemic, so some recommendations might not seem actionable very soon. However, the crisis also presents a unique opportunity to further develop the proposed initiatives to be launched in 2021 and beyond.

Appendixes

Appendix 1. Country Consultations

➢ Azerbaijan and Georgia

The Azerbaijan–Georgia border was selected for a field mission because these two countries are part of the Eastern Partnership Territorial Cooperation Support Programme, funded by the European Union (EU). Valuable lessons can be drawn from the EU approach to cross-border community development. The Eastern Partnership Territorial Cooperation (EAPTC) is a joint policy initiative aiming at deepening and strengthening relations between the EU, its member states, and its six eastern neighbors: Armenia, Azerbaijan, Belarus, Georgia, Moldova, and Ukraine.

The Central Asia Regional Economic Cooperation (CAREC) team met the Deutsche Gesellschaft für Internationale Zusammenarbeit (GIZ), the implementing agency of EAPTC in Georgia and Azerbaijan. Some of the lessons learned include the following:

(i)   Regional cooperation initiatives need to align with central government policies, and national and local administrations need support.

(ii) Donor fund disbursement mechanisms need to be adopted to the national and international transfer of funds regulations.

(iii) Regional cooperation experience exchange is useful to promote stakeholders' networking, including information campaigns for beneficiaries.

(iv) Initiatives fostering people-to-people contacts and integration are effective, although the operating environment is strict.

EAPTC implemented six projects in the Azerbaijan–Georgia border.

Eastern Partnership Territorial Cooperation Projects Implemented in the Azerbaijan–Georgia Border

EAPTC Main Beneficiary (Lead Partner)	EAPTC Project Name
Union of Azerbaijani Women of Georgia	Youth Empowerment through Living Values[a]
Koda Community Education Center	Civil Society for Development and Cooperation: Increasing Tourism Potential in the Bordering Regions of Azerbaijan and Georgia[b]
Civil Development	Young Entrepreneurs Synergy (YES!)[c]
Ganja Agribusiness Association	Introducing Environmentally Friendly Pest-Control for Bio-Protection of Agricultural Crops in the Border Areas[d]

continued on next page

Appendix 1 table *continued*

EAPTC Main Beneficiary (Lead Partner)	EAPTC Project Name
Ganja Euro-Atlantic Information Center Public Union	Strengthening the Cross-Border Partnership in Provision of New Social Services for Children with Disabilities in Ganja-Gazakh region of Azerbaijan and Kvemo Kartli region of Georgia[e]
Telavi Municipality Assembly	Employability Skills for Young People[f]

[a] EAPTC. 2018. *Youth Empowerment through Living Values.* The project aimed to empower young people living in the cross-border regions to promote positive social changes and meaningful cooperation by creating life value school-based centers and celebrating joint culture, sports, and tourism events.
[b] EAPTC. 2018. *Civil Society for Development and Cooperation: Increasing Tourism Potential in the Bordering Regions of Azerbaijan and Georgia.*
[c] EAPTC. 2018. *Young Entrepreneurs Synergy (YES!) Network for Georgia–Azerbaijan Cross-Border Cooperation.*
[d] EAPTC. 2018. *Introducing Environmentally Friendly Pest-Control for Bio-Protection of Agricultural Crops in the Border Areas of Azerbaijan (Sheki-Zagatala) and Georgia (Lagodekhi).*
[e] EAPTC. 2018. *Strengthening the Cross-Border Partnership in Provision of New Social Services for Children with Disabilities in Ganja-Gazakh region of Azerbaijan and Kvemo Kartli Region of Georgia.*
[f] EAPTC. 2018. *Employability Skills for Young People in Sheki and Telavi Municipality.*

EAPTC = Eastern Partnership Territorial Cooperation.

Source: Eastern Partnership Territorial Cooperation (EAPTC). 2018. Eastern Partnership Territorial Cooperation Support Programme.

The mission also met private sector-related agencies such as the Chamber of Commerce, aside from the beneficiaries or lead partners above. The findings from these meetings have been included in the study.

➢ People's Republic of China and Mongolia

The border area between the People's Republic of China (PRC) and Mongolia has been selected to hold some field consultations, given that both countries upgraded bilateral ties to a comprehensive strategic partnership in 2014. Economic cooperation between these two countries prioritizes natural resources and infrastructure. This partnership also aims to increase political communication to strengthen security cooperation. In 2014, the Belt and Road Initiative supported the PRC–Mongolia–Russian Federation Economic Corridor to establish free trade and economic cooperation zones in cross-border cities between these countries.[1]

Meetings in Ulaanbaatar included (i) the Confucius Institute at National University of Mongolia; (ii) the Mongolian National Chamber of Commerce and Industry; (iii) the Ministry of Nature, Environment and Tourism of Mongolia; (iv) the World Bank; and (v) the Partnership for Action on Green Economy in Mongolia.

Meetings in Inner Mongolia Autonomous Region, PRC included (i) the Inner Mongolia Autonomous Region Department of Transport, (ii) the China Council for the Promotion of International Trade, and (iii) the Erenhot Cross-Border Economic Cooperation Zone.

➢ Tajikistan

During their mission to Tajikistan on 21–26 May 2018, the Asian Development Bank (ADB) team met with the following donors and implementing partners of cross-border programs: Aga Khan Development Network (AKDN), Japan International Cooperation Agency, KfW Development Bank, United Nations

---

[1] Y. Chen. 2018. China and Japan's Investment Competition in Mongolia. *The Diplomat.* 1 August.

Development Programme (UNDP), University of Central Asia, Association of Entrepreneurs and Mountain Farmers, Kyrgyzstan Mountain Societies Development Support Programme, Aga Khan Health Services, Roof of the World Festival, and cross-border traders. Field observations of the cross-border program activities were also conducted during the ADB mission's field visit.

The team also met with the country heads of the Aga Khan Foundation, JICA, KfW, and UNDP in Dushanbe to learn from their cross-border programming before embarking on a 4-day field visit to Khatlon and Gorno-Badakhshan Autonomous Oblast to see the cross-border interventions implemented by the partners.

The findings from these meetings have been included in the study.

Appendix 2. Visa-Entry Arrangements between CAREC Countries

From→ To↓	AFG	AZE	PRC	GEO	KAZ	KGZ	MON	PAK	TAJ	TKM	UZB
AFG		C	C	C	C	C	C	C	C	C	C
AZE	C		A / B	F	F	F	C	B	F	B	F
PRC	C	C		C	C [a]	C	F	C	C	C	C
GEO	C	F	B		F	F	B	C	F	F	F
KAZ	C	F	B / C	F		F	F	C	F	C	F
KGZ	B	F	B	F	F		F	B	F	B	F
MON	C	C	C	C	F	F		C	C	C	C
PAK	C	A / B	B	B	B	B	B		A / B	B	B
TAJ	B	F	B	F	F	F	C	B		A / B	F
TKM	C	C	A / C	C	C	C	C	C	C		C
UZB	B	F	F	F	F	F	F	B	F	B	

AFG = Afghanistan, AZE = Azerbaijan, CAREC = Central Asia Regional Economic Cooperation, PRC = People's Republic of China, GEO = Georgia, KAZ = Kazakhstan, KGZ = Kyrgyz Republic, MON = Mongolia, PAK= Pakistan, TAJ = Tajikistan, TKM = Turkmenistan, UZB = Uzbekistan.

Notes:

1. A = visa on arrival, B = eligible for e-visa, C = visa required prior to travel, F = visa-free.

2. All results relate to ordinary passport holders.

[a] Free entry for Kazakhstan into Hainan Province, PRC.

Source: Passport Index. Compare Passports (accessed 1 July 2020).

Appendix 3. Main Border Crossing Points between CAREC Countries

Country 1	Country 2	Extension of Border (km)	#	Name of Crossing Point	Location in Country 1	Location in Country 2	Ethnic Groups	Additional Information
AZE	GEO	480	1	Red Bridge (Tsiteli Khidi)	Gazakh region, Shikhli II village	Kvemo Kartli region, Marneuli district, village Kerch-Muganlo	Georgians: 217,305 (51.25%)	These five cross-border points allow all types of passengers and goods. The mining industry is important in bordering regions between Georgia and Azerbaijan. Bordering markets gather agricultural and handicraft products.
			2	Sadikhli (AZE) or Vakhtangisi (GEO)	Agstafa region, Sadikhli village	Kvemo Kartli region, Vakhtangisi village	Azerbaijanis: 177,032 (41.75%)	
			3	Balakan (AZE) or Lagodekhi (GEO)	Balakan region	Kakheti region, Lagodekhi district, village Matsimi	Armenians: 21,500 (5.07%)	
			4	Mughanlo (AZE) or Samtatskaro (GEO)	Gazakh region	Dedoplistskaro Municipality, village Samtatskaro	Greeks: 2,631 (0.62%)	
			5	Almali (AZE) or Gardabani (GEO)	Gazakh region	Marneuli Municipality, village Sadakhlo–Railway Station	Russians: 2,113 (0.49%)	The Almali or Gardabani is a railway crossing point.
	PRC	76	1	Wakhjir Pass	Mountain range	Mountain range	–	These two passes are closed owing to the closure of Chalachigu Valley to visitors on the PRC side. Access is allowed for residents and herders living in the area.
			2	Tegermansu Pass	Mountain range	Mountain range	–	
AFG	PAK	2,430	1	Torkham (Khyber Pass and Momand Dara district)	Jalalabad, Nangahar	Peshawar	Balochi, Sindhi, and Pashtun are major tribes with several smaller tribes such as Utmankhel, Mohmand, Tarkani, and Safi.	There are 18 unofficial motorable crossings and around 235 navigable crossings. There are eight official border crossing points between Afghanistan and Pakistan. Torkham and Spin Boldak crossing points have an international status. The rest are bilateral: Arandu (Chitral), Gursal (Bajaur), Nawa Pass (Mohmand), Kharlachi (Kurram), Ghulam Khan (North Waziristan), Angoor Adda (South Waziristan), and Chaman (Balochistan).
			2	Spin Boldak (Wesh–Chaman)	Kandahar province	Quetta, Balochistan		
			3	Ghulam Khan	Gurbaz, Khost	Miranshah, North Waziristan		
	TAJ	1,206	1	Shir Khan Bandar (AFG) – Panji Poyon (TAJ)	Kunduz	Kumsangir district	Tajiks, Turkmens, and Uzbeks	Numerous settlements can be found on both sides of this border. The Afghanistan side include Baghri Kol, Kolukh Teppe, Shir Khan Bandar, Shah Ravan, Chichkeh Dasht-e-Qala, Kvahan, Khosfav, Arakhat, and Ishkashim. On the Tajikistan side, we can find Ayvadzh, Panji Poyon, Dusty, Panj, Parkhar, Kishti Royen, Qal'ai Khumb, Kevron, Rushon, Bazhdu Pavdiv, Khorugh, Ishkoshim, and Sinib.

continued on next page

Appendix 3 table *continued*

Country 1	Country 2	Extension of Border (km)	#	Name of Crossing Point	Location in Country 1	Location in Country 2	Ethnic Groups	Additional Information
AFG (cont.)	TAJ		2	Sultan Highway (AFG) or Ishkashim Highway (TAJ)	Badakhshan	Ishkashim district	Tajiks, Turkmens, and Uzbeks	Dasht-e-Qala, Kvahan, Khosfav, Arakhat, and Ishkashim. In Tajikistan, these include Ayvadzh, Panji Poyon, Dusty, Panj, Parkhar, Kishti Royen, Qal'ai Khumb, Kevron, Rushon, Bazhdu Pavdiv, Khorugh, Ishkoshim, and Sinib.
	TKM	744	1	Torghundi (AFG) – Serkhetabat (TKM) (road and rail)	Herat Koshk (Administration Herat)	Yoloten		There are several settlements near the Afghanistan border, including Murichaq, Jalajin, Muhammad Tashi, Soltan Robat, Yaka Haji, Bai Khan, Kawk, Khamyab, Qarqin, and Keleft. Settlements such as Serhetabat, Bashbeden, Khodzhali, Ymamnazar, and Bosaga can be found on the Turkmenistan side of this border.
			2	Aqina (AFG) – Ymamnazar (TKM) (rail)	Faryab Province	Lebap province		
	UZB	137	1	Hairatan (AFG)– Termez (UZB) (road)	Balkh Province	Termez region		The river Amu Darya divides the two countries.
			2	Hairatan (AFG) – Galaba (UZB) (rail)				Settlements near the border in Afghanistan are Dali, Kaldar, and Hairatan. On the Uzbekistan side is Termez.
PRC	KAZ	1,533	1	Khorgos/ Nur Zholy	Urumqi	Almaty	PRC: Uighurs, Kazakhs, and Han Chinese KAZ: Kazakh	Since 2018, the former Khorgos border crossing is no longer active and now only functions as a special economic zone.
			2	Maikapchagai– Jeminay	Xinjiang Uygur Autonomous Region	North Kazakhstan		The Khorgos International Center for Boundary Cooperation opened in 2011 and is a visa-free zone. Residents from both sides of the border can trade and enjoy local entertainment.[a]
			3	Bakhty–Tacheng	Tacheng	Bakhty		Settlements near the border in the PRC include Tacheng, Huocheng, and Khorgos. In Kazakhstan, these include Alekseyeva, Taunchang, Akshoky, Bakhty, Dostyk, Almaly, Khorgos, Kolzhat, Sarybastau, Sumbe, and Narynkol.
			4	Dostyk/Druzhba– Alashankou	Alashankou	Dostyk		
			5	Qaljat (Kalzhat)– Dulata Port	Qaljat	Dulata		

continued on next page

Appendix 3 table *continued*

Country 1	Country 2	Extension of Border (km)	#	Name of Crossing Point	Location in Country 1	Location in Country 2	Ethnic Groups	Additional Information
PRC (cont.)	KGZ	858	1	Irkeshtam Pass: Osh–Kashgar	Kashgar	Osh	KGZ: Tajiks, Kyrgyz Germans	Kashgar has historically served as a trading center and was once a major hub along the Silk Road.[b] The city was made into a special economic zone in 2010, the only city in western PRC with this distinction.
			2	Torugart Pass	Xinjiang Uygur Autonomous Region	Naryn province	PRC: Uighurs Kyrgyz, and Han Chinese	
	MON	4,677	1	Erenhot–Zamyn-Uud Cross-Border Economic Cooperation Zone	Erenhot	Zamyn-Uud	PRC: Hans and Mongols MON: Mongols	The bordering towns of Erenhot and Zamyn-Uud have become a rail port city and the largest hub for cross-border trade between the PRC and Mongolia. When this Economic Cooperation Zone opened in 1922 to international trade, Erenhot's population increased from 8,000 to 100,000, inluding labor migrants. As Bulgan–Takashiken or Bichigt Zuun–Khatavch, there are other borders mainly used to export minerals, such as Khangi-Mandal, Sumber–Rashaan, Bayankhoshuu-Uvdug, Khavirgaa–Arkhashaat, and Gashuun Sukhait–Gants Mod.
			2	Bulgan – Takashiken	Takashiken, PRC	Bulgan soum, Khovd province		
			3	Bichigt Zuun–Khatavch	Zuun Uzemchin Khoshuu, Xiliin Gol, Inner Mongolia Autonomous Region	Erdenetsagaan soum, Sukhbaatar province		
			4	Sheveekhuren – Sekhee	Eznee, Alshaa, Inner Mongolia Autonomous Region	Gurvantes, Umnugovi province		This border post is closed for tourists and used for coal exports from Mongolia to the PRC.
			5	Sumber – Arxa/ Aershan	Rashaan town, Hyangan, Inner Mongolia Autonomous Region	Khalkhgol soum, Dornod province	–	–
	PAK	438	1	Khunjerab Pass	Sinkiang	Hunza, Nagar	PRC: Uighurs and Han Chinese PAK: Shins, Yashkuns, Kashmiris, Kashgaris, Pamiris, Pathans, and Kohistanis	–
	TAJ	477	1	Kulma Pass (Karasu Pass)	Taxkorgan Tajik Autonomous County, Kashgar Prefecture, Xinjiang Uygur Autonomous Region	Murghob district, Gorno-Badakhshan Autonomous Region	PRC. Uighurs and Han Chinese Turkic peoples also include Tatars. TAJ: Tajiks	–

continued on next page

Appendix 3 table *continued*

Country 1	Country 2	Extension of Border (km)	#	Name of Crossing Point	Location in Country 1	Location in Country 2	Ethnic Groups	Additional Information
KAZ	KGZ	1,212	1	Korday	Korday, Jambyl region	Lugovoye/Akjol	Kyrgyz and Kazakhs	Some border crossings are for locals only, such as Alatau (a hiking path from Almaty to Lake Issyk-Kul), Kenbulun, and Sartobe. Settlements near the border in Kazakhstan include Taraz, Kasyk, and Korday. On the Kyrgyz Republic border, these include Kök-Say, Amanbayevo, Sheker, Pokrovka, Kyzyl-Adyr, Köpürö-Bazar, Chaldybar, Chuy, Kaindy, Kamyshanovka, Vasil'yevka, Birdik, Ivanovka, Tokmok, Kara-Bulak, and Tüp.
			2	Karasu (KAZ) or Ak-Tilek (KGZ)	Karasu, Jambyl region	Ak-Tilek		
			3	Kegen	Kegen, Almaty region	Tup/Kensu		
			4	Aisha Bibi–Chon-Kapka	Taraz, Jambyl region	Talasz		
			5	Sypatay Batyr	Sypatay, Jambyl region	Batyr		
			6	Chaldovar	Jambyl region	–	–	Chaldovar crossing point is a railway cargo-passenger checkpoint.
	TKM	413	1	Zhanaozen–Garabogaz	Zhanaozen	Garabogaz	Kazakhs and Turkmen	Garabogaz is a settlement near the border on the Turkmenistan side.
			2	Bolashak–Serkhetyaka	Bolashak	Serkhetyaka		
	UZB	2,330	1	Zhibek–Joly–Gisht Kupric	Turkestan region	Tashkent region	Turkestan region: Kazakhs: 76.02% Uzbeks: 16.97% Tajiks :1.86% Russians: 1.79% Others: 3.36% Tashkent region: Uzbeks: 82.0% Russians: 6.0% Koryo-saram (Koreans): 5% Kazakhs: 2% Tajiks: 2% Tatars: 2% Others: 1%	Settlements near the Kazakhstan border include Chabankazgan, Shardara, Zhetisay, Myrzakent, Atakent, and Saryagash. Settlements in the Uzbekistan side include Karakalpakiya, Gagarin, Guliston, Baxt, Sirdaryo, Chinaz, Yangiyo'l, Tashkent, Keles, Chirchiq, and Gazalkent.
			2	Tejen–Daut Ata	Mangystau region (Beyneu)	Karakalpakstan (Kungrad)		
			3	Yalama–Konysbayeva	Turkestan region	Tashkent region (Chinaz district)		
			4	Serke–Turkistan (Kazygurt)–Tashkent	Turkestan region	Tashkent region		
			5	Kaplanbek–Zangiota	Turkestan region	Tashkent region		
			6	Atamaken–Gulistan	Turkestan region	Sirdarya region		
			7	Celinny–Ak Oltin	Turkestan region	Sirdarya region		
			8	Sirdarya–Malik	Turkestan region	Sirdarya region		

continued on next page

Appendix 3 table *continued*

Country 1	Country 2	Extension of Border (km)	#	Name of Crossing Point	Location in Country 1	Location in Country 2	Ethnic Groups	Additional Information
KGZ	TAJ	984	1	Batken – Isfara	Batken	Isfara	–	Settlements near the border on the Kyrgyz Republic side can be found at Batken, Samarkandyk, Tsentralnoye, Kulundu, Sulukta, Samat, Ak-Suu, Kök-Tash, Kara-Teyit, Karamyk, and Bor-Doba. In Tajikistan, settlements near the border can be found at Lakkon, Kulkent, Navgilem, Isfara, Surkh, Chorku, Shurab, Qistaquz, Ghafurov, Proletarsk, Mujum, Dakhkat, and Rosrovut.
			2	Kulundu – Ovchi Kalacha	Kulundu	Ovchi Kalacha	–	
			3	Madaniyat – Madaniyay	Madaniyat	Madaniyay	–	
			4	Karamyk – Daroot Korgan	Karamyk	Daroot Korgan	–	
			5	Bor-Doba – Kyzylart	Bor-Doba	Kyzylart	–	
	UZB	1,314	1	Dostyk-Dostlik	Osh region	Andijon region	More than half of all the Kyrgyz Republic's Uzbeks live in Osh region, 28% of the regional population.	Settlements near the Kyrgyz Republic border include Kёk-Tash, Sumsar, Ala-Buka, Akkorgon, Ak-Tam, Tuyukdzhar, Kerben, Uspenkovka, Kyzyl-Jar, Shamaldy-Say, Kochkor-Ata, Jalal-Abad, Kara-Suu, Osh, Aravan, Uch-Korgon, Kyzyl-Kiya Kadamjay, Pulgon, and Zar-Tash. Near Uzbekistan, these include Gava, Varzik, Kosonsoy, Iskavat, Zarkent, Paramat, Bekovat, Yangikurgan, Uchqo'rg'on, Paytug, Andijan, Paxtaobod, Dardak, Khanabad, Qorasuv, Qo'rg'ontepa, Asaka (Uzbekistan), Palvantash, Marhamat, Quva, Fergana, Quvasoy, Margilan and Rishton.
			2	Bekabad-Khanobad	Jalal-Abad region	Andijon region		
			3	Madaniyat-Madaniyat	Jalal-Abad region	Andijon region		
			4	Kizil-Kiya–Uzbekistan	Batken region	Fergana region		
			5	Kensay-Uchkurgan	Jalal-Abad region	Namangan region		
			6	Kara-Bagish–Mingtepa	Osh region	Andijon region		
			7	Baymak-Kasansoy	Jalal-Abad region	Namangan region		
			8	Seydukum-Pushmon	Jalal-Abad region	Andijon region		
			9	Intimak-Keakaner	Osh region	Andijon region		
			10	Sumsar-Karakurgan	Jalal-Abad region	Namangan region		

continued on next page

Appendix 3 table *continued*

Country 1	Country 2	Extension of Border (km)	#	Name of Crossing Point	Location in Country 1	Location in Country 2	Ethnic Groups	Additional Information
TAJ	UZB	1,312	1	Aivaj-Gulbakhor	Khatlon region	Surkhandarya region	Tajik, Uzbek	Settlements near the border on the Tajikistan side can be found at Lakkon, Kulkent, Navgilem, Isfara, Konibodom, Punuk, Jarbulak, Paldorak, Buston, Mastchoh, Kuruksoi, Obburdon, Farmonkurgon, Zafarobod, Mehnatobod, Istaravshan, Shahriston, Panjakent, Farob, Pakhtaobod, and Tursunzoda. On the Uzbekistan side, settlements are at Olmaliq, Bekabad, Khavast, Ulyanovo, Urgut, and Denov. Bilateral crossings include Bekobod/Kushtegirmon, between Khujand and Gulistan; Pap-Novbunyod, between Khujand and Namangan; and Khavastabad, Uchturgan, and Qushkent in Sughd province.
			2	Bratstvo-Sariasiya	Tursunzoda	Surkhandarya region		
			3	Fatehabad–Oybek	Soghd region	Tashkent region		
			4	Patar-Anderkhan	Soghd region	Fergana region		
			5	Sarazm-Jartepa	Soghd region	Samarkand region		
			6	Rawat	Soghd region	Fergana region		
			7	Khashtyak-Bekabad	Soghd region	Sirdarya region		
			8	Novbunyod-Pap	Soghd region	Namangan region		
			9	Kushtegirmon-Plotina	Soghd region	Tashkent region		
			10	Zafarabad-Khavasabad	Soghd region	Sirdarya region		
			11	Khavatog-Uchkurgan	Soghd region	Jizzakh region		
			12	Urta-Tepa–Kushkent	Soghd region	Jizzakh region		
TKM	UZB	1,621	1	Farap-Alat	Lebap region	Bukhara region	Turkmen, Uzbek	Settlements near the border on the Turkmenistan side can be found at Kunya-Urgench, Takhiadash, Dashoguz, Gasojak, Dargan Ata, Turkmenabat, Farap. On the Uzbekistan side, settlements are at Shumany, Khojaly, Takhiadash, Shovot, Mangit, Yablykangly, Gazavat, Khiva, Hazorasp, Pitnak, and Olot.
			2	Telimerjen-Talimarjan	Lebap region	Kashkadaryo region		
			3	Gasojak-Drujba	Lebap region	Khorezm region		
			4	Doshoguz-Shavat	Doshoguz region	Khorezm region		
			5	Kunya-Urgench-Khujayli	Doshoguz region	Karakalpakstan		
			6	Farap-Khojadavlet	Lebap region	Bukhara region		

AFG = Afghanistan, AZE = Azerbaijan, PRC = People's Republic of China, GEO = Georgia, KAZ = Kazakhstan, KGZ = Kyrgyz Republic, km = kilometer, MON = Mongolia, PAK = Pakistan, TAJ = Tajikistan, TKM = Turkmenistan, UZB = Uzbekistan.

Note: Countries are ordered alphabetically, and each border appears only once.

[a] D. Trilling. 2014. On China–Kazakhstan Border Lies a Lopsided Free-Trade Zone. *Eurasianet*. 5 September.

[b] United Nations Educational, Scientific and Cultural Organization. Silk Roads Programme: Kashgar.

Source: CAREC Secretariat.

Bibliography

Abdullaev, I., J. Kazbekov, H. Manthrithilake, and K. Jumaboev. 2009. Water User Groups in Central Asia: Emerging Form of Collective Action in Irrigation Water Management. *Water Resources Management*. 24 (5). pp. 1029–1043.

Afghan Studies Center. Pak-Afghan Youth Dialogue Series.

Asian Development Bank (ADB). 2017. *CAREC 2030: Connecting the Region for Shared and Sustainable Development*. Manila.

——. 2019. *Education and Skills Development under the CAREC Program: Scoping Study*. Manila.

——. 2019. *Promoting Regional Tourism Cooperation under CAREC 2030: A Scoping Study*. Manila.

——. Draft CAREC Gender Strategy 2030. Unpublished.

CGTN. 2018. Retracking the Ancient Silk Road: Ulanqab: New Future for the Old Caravansaries. 4 October.

Chappelow, J. 2020. Eurasian Economic Union (EAEU). *Investopedia*. 18 September.

Chen, Y. 2018. China and Japan's Investment Competition in Mongolia. *The Diplomat*. 1 August.

China Daily. 2014. China, Mongolia Upgrade Ties to Comprehensive Strategic Partnership. 21 August.

China Daily. 2019. Tea Road Cultural Tourism Expo Opens in Ulaanqab. 24 June.

Chirisa, I., O. S. Dirwai, and A. Mumba. 2014. A Review of the Evolution and Trajectory of the African Union as an Instrument of Regional Integration. *SpringerPlus*. 2014 (3). pp. 101–114.

Coccossis, H. and P. Nijkamp. 2012. Overcoming Isolation: Information and Transportation Networks in Development Strategies for Peripheral Areas. In *Advances in Spatial Science*. Springer Science & Business Media. p. 55.

Cornell, S. E. and S. F. Starr. 2018. Regional Cooperation in Central Asia: Relevance of World Models. *The Central Asia-Caucasus Analyst*. 4 December.

Deutsche Gesellschaft für Internationale Zusammenarbeit (GIZ). Eastern Partnership Territorial Cooperation within the Context of the Local Governance Programme South Caucasus.

Eastern Partnership Territorial Cooperation (EAPTC). 2018. *Azerbaijan–Georgia Joint Operational Programme.*

———. 2018. *Eastern Partnership Territorial Cooperation Support Programme.*

Free and Fair Election Network. 2019. *Peaceful, Well-Managed Elections in Newly Merged Districts Mark Completion of Constitutional Merger.*

Hasanli, I. 2018. *Country Report: Azerbaijan Borders. Centre for National and International Studies.*

Kakubava, N. and T. Chincharauli. 2010. *Cross-Border Cooperation: Practical Guide.* Association of Young Economists of Georgia.

Mackay, A. 2008. Border Management and Gender. In Megan Bastick and Kristin Valasek, eds. *Gender and Security Sector Reform Toolkit.* Geneva: DCAF, OSCE/ODIHR, UN-INSTRAW.

Matthews, A. 2003. Regional Integration in Africa. In *Regional Integration and Food Security in Developing Countries.* Food and Agriculture Organization of the United Nations. Rome.

Medeiros, E. 2018. *European Territorial Cooperation: Theoretical and Empirical Approaches to the Process and Impacts of Cross-Border and Transnational Cooperation in Europe.* Springer International Publishing.

Morel, A. 2020. Afghanistan's Borderlands: Unruly, Unruled, and Central to Peace. *The Asia Foundation.* 22 January.

Russia Business Today. 2019. Russia to Boost Tourism Links to China, Mongolia. 24 June.

Schengen Visa Info. Schengen Area.

Slusarciuc, M. 2013. Partnership and Cooperation Models in Cross-Border Areas. *AUDŒ.* 9 (4). pp. 267–280.

Umotbay uulu, D. 2018. A Day at the Largest Market of Fergana Valley. *Central Asian Bureau for Analytical Reporting.* 17 October.

United Nations Development Programme (UNDP). Border Management in Northern Afghanistan II (BOMNAF II).

———. Development of Red Bridge Border Crossing Point between Georgia and Azerbaijan.

UN Women. 2017. *Women Forge Peace along the Kyrgyz-Tajik Border.* Stories. 2 February.

University of Central Asia. 2019. Kyrgyz Republic: Current Dynamics of the Border Areas in the Fergana Valley Workshop. 14 February.

Warren, H. S., M. Liungman, and A. Yang. 2019. *What's It Like for Women to Trade across Borders? World Bank Blog.* 3 June.

Weijer, F. de. 2017. *Review of PBF Cross-Border Cooperation for Sustainable Peace and Development.* PeaceNexus Foundation.

Wilton-Steer, C. 2018. Reconnecting Afghan & Tajik Badakhshan: Economic Development in the Cross-Border Region. *Aga Khan Foundation UK.* 19 December.

World Bank. 2018. *Project information Document/ Integrated Safeguards Data Sheet: Uzbekistan Prosperous Villages.* 10 September.

———. 2019. Ferghana Valley Rural Enterprise Development Project.

World Economic Forum. 2019. *Climate Change Is Threatening Security in Central Asia. Here Are Ways to Reduce the Risk.* 25 January.

Xinhuanet. 2019. Factbox: New Progress in Pursuit of Belt and Road Initiative. 19 March.

Xinhuanet. 2020. Mongolia–China Trade Volume Reaches 8.9 Bln USD in 2019. 26 January.

Zhe, H. 2019. China, Russia, and Mongolia Meet to Reinforce Trilateral Tourism Ties. *Chinadaily.* 24 June.

Zhou, R. 2019. The Mongol Minority. *China Highlights.* 17 January.